COTEACHING
IN TEACHER EDUCATION

Innovative pedagogy for excellence

Critical Guides for
Teacher Educators

You might also like the following books from Critical Publishing.

Ability Grouping in Primary Schools: Case Studies and Critical Debates
Rachel Marks
978-1-910391-24-2

Beginning Teachers' Learning: Making Experience Count
Katharine Burn, Hazel Hagger and Trevor Mutton
978-1-910391-17-4

Developing Creative and Critical Educational Practitioners
Victoria Door
978-1-909682-37-5

Developing Outstanding Practice in School-based Teacher Education
Edited by Kim Jones and Elizabeth White
978-1-909682-41-2

How Do Expert Primary Classteachers Really Work? A Critical Guide for Teachers, Headteachers and Teacher Educators
Tony Eaude
978-1-909330-01-6

Post-Compulsory Teacher Educators: Connecting Professionals
Edited by Jim Crawley
978-1-910391-86-0

Teacher Status and Professional Learning: The Place Model
Linda Clarke
978-1-910391-46-4

Theories of Professional Learning
Carey Philpott
978-1-909682-33-7

Our titles are also available in a range of electronic formats. To order please go to our website www.criticalpublishing.com or contact our distributor NBN International by telephoning 01752 202301 or emailing orders@nbninternational.com.

COTEACHING
IN TEACHER EDUCATION

Innovative pedagogy for excellence

Series Editor: Ian Menter

Critical Guides for
Teacher Educators

Colette Murphy

First published in 2016 by Critical Publishing Ltd

British Library Cataloguing in Publication Data
A CIP record for this book is available from the British Library

ISBN: 978-1-910391-82-2

This book is also available in the following e-book formats:
MOBI: 978-1-910391-83-9
EPUB: 978-1-910391-84-6
Adobe e-book reader: 978-1-910391-85-3

Cover and text design by Greensplash Limited
Project Management by Out of House Publishing
Typeset by Newgen Knowledge Works Pvt. Ltd.
Print Managed and Manufactured by Jellyfish Solutions

Critical Publishing
3 Connaught Road
St Albans
AL3 5RX

www.criticalpublishing.com

CONTENTS

ACKNOWLEDGEMENTS

This book has been written as a guide to coteaching for teacher educators. I would like to acknowledge the Primary Science Teaching Trust (PSTT) for their generous funding of coteaching research in primary science carried out in Northern Ireland. I'd also like to thank Jim Beggs, my fellow coteacher from the beginning, who has also helped me enormously with writing this book. Finally, my thanks go to Julia Morris, Ian Menter, and all the Critical Publishing team, for their encouragement and support throughout.

FOREWORD

Since launching the series *Critical Guides for Teacher Educators* in 2014, the need for such volumes seems to have increased yet more. When we started the series we were acutely aware that there were many parts of the world where teacher education was becoming increasingly diverse in its organisation, structure and curriculum. Furthermore, an increasing range of participants were being asked to take responsibility for supporting the introduction of new members into the profession and for ensuring their continuing learning and development. It is certainly my belief that earlier volumes in the series have helped enormously in providing the kinds of research-based insights that will support the development of high-quality teacher learning and development in whatever context it is taking place.

The books have always been cognisant of the benefits of international research and experience in teacher education and are being well received in many parts of the world. Their emphasis on criticality is also very important in today's world where politicians often promulgate simple, indeed simplistic, answers to the 'policy problem' of teacher education.

We can see how important such work is when we read global overviews of teacher education policy and practice such as that provided by Darling-Hammond and Lieberman (2012). But we can also see how rich the context of the United Kingdom and the Republic of Ireland is, when analysing what is happening in the five nations: England, Northern Ireland, Scotland, Wales and the Republic of Ireland, as demonstrated in the recent work *Teacher Education in Times of Change* (Teacher Education Group, 2016).

Similarly, the widely cited report of the inquiry undertaken by the British Educational Research Association (BERA) in collaboration with the Royal Society for the Arts, Manufacture and Commerce (RSA) (BERA-RSA, 2014) has offered evidence for the importance of a systematic approach to the use of research and evidence in high-quality teacher education.

It is therefore a great pleasure to introduce Colette Murphy's volume to the series. Colette is a leading advocate of coteaching, the teacher education practice that she examines closely in this volume. Coteaching has many of the important features that are evident internationally in good teacher education practice – it is fundamentally a collaborative approach and is based on well-established pedagogical principles, derived in large part from the work of the Soviet researcher Lev Vygotsky. It involves the systematic deployment of these principles in classrooms where pre-service and established teachers can collaborate in supporting each other's professional learning. The research that Colette has herself undertaken, as well as that of others which she reports, also demonstrates clearly how coteaching has had a positive effect on the learning outcomes of pupils. Much of Colette's work has taken place in the Republic of Ireland and is being supported by the Teaching Council there, demonstrating how a European state can provide a lead in the consolidation of effective professional practice in teacher education, that could well be followed by practitioners and policymakers elsewhere, including in these islands. But as alluded to earlier, the volume also makes extensive reference to work carried out internationally, including particularly significant developments in the USA. The book concludes with a fascinating argument for the relevance of coteaching to pedagogical development in the twenty-first century, which Colette characterises as a time of a 'postmodern', 'knowledge society'.

Ian Menter, Series Editor
Emeritus Professor of Teacher Education, University of Oxford

References

BERA-RSA (2014) *Research and the Teaching Profession – Building Capacity for a Self-improving Education System.* London: BERA. [online] Available at: www.bera.ac.uk/wp-content/uploads/2013/12/BERA-RSA-Research-Teaching-Profession-FULL-REPORT-for-web.pdf (accessed September 2016).

Darling-Hammond, L and Lieberman, A (eds) (2012) *Teacher Education around the World.* London: Routledge.

The Teacher Education Group (2016) *Teacher Education in Times of Change.* Bristol: Policy Press.

About the series editor

Ian Menter is Emeritus Professor of Teacher Education and was formerly the Director of Professional Programmes in the Department of Education at the University of Oxford. He previously worked at the Universities of Glasgow, the West of Scotland, London Metropolitan, the West of England and Gloucestershire. Before that he was a primary school teacher in Bristol, England. His most recent publications include *A Literature Review on Teacher Education for the 21st Century* (Scottish Government) and *A Guide to Practitioner Research in Education* (Sage). His work has also been published in many academic journals.

About the author

Colette Murphy is a professor of science and mathematics education at the School of Education, Trinity College Dublin. She has been a teacher educator for more than 25 years and has published two books and many articles on improving the experience of pre-service teachers in schools. Her research centres on science learning and teaching at all levels and she is widely published in this area. Most specifically, she is well known for her work on coteaching in initial teacher education, and for her expertise in Vygotsky and science learning. She is a Vygotsky scholar and is in the process of writing a biography of Lev Semenovich Vygotsky (1896–1934). Her current research is grounded mostly in a neo-Vygotskian perspective, which focuses on learner agency.

> ## CRITICAL **ISSUES**
>
> - *What is coteaching, and what is its potential for improving initial and in-service teacher education?*
> - *What does coteaching look like in the classroom?*
> - *How does coteaching differ from other forms of collaborative teaching?*

Introduction

Coteaching serves as pedagogy to improve school-based experience for pre-service and in-service teachers. In coteaching, pre-service teachers (PSTs) and in-service teachers (ISTs) plan, teach and evaluate a series of lessons together (usually eight to ten). Coteaching has changed the face of pre-service teaching, which, it is argued, does not equip new teachers sufficiently well for twenty-first century classroom teaching (a good overview is presented in Bacharach, Heck and Dahlberg, 2010a). Currently, almost 40 per cent of teachers in the UK drop out within a year of qualifying (Weale, 2015). Attrition among new teachers is an international problem; reasons include isolation, pressure to be 'outstanding', excessive home-based workload and managing pupil misbehaviour. Other issues for new teachers in the UK reported recently by Weale (2016) are long hours, endless administration, angry parents, poorly planned change, constant criticism and the stress of Ofsted visits. Such increasing demands upon new teachers make many of them feel ill-equipped to take on the role when they start as a full-time teacher. The traditional practice in school experience for PSTs comprises a period of observation followed by complete takeover of classes. This practice has not changed in more than a century, despite significant developments in the role of a teacher, the needs of pupils, the learning environment and the functioning of schools. With coteaching, PSTs gain confidence rapidly, working alongside ISTs. ISTs gain both professional development and an expanded repertoire of teaching approaches and resources.

Sharing of ideas, experience and expertise lies at the root of coteaching, as PST and IST work together in coplanning, copractice and coevaluating for a short series of lessons during school-based experience. Coteaching bridges observation and solo teaching and develops coteachers' confidence as they share expertise and coreflect on their progress towards providing 'ideal' learning environments for pupils. Words ascribed to George Bernard Shaw illustrate the difference between sharing resources and sharing ideas, or expertise.

If you have an apple and I have an apple and we exchange these apples then you and I will still each have one apple. But if you have an idea and I have an idea and we exchange these ideas, then each of us will have two ideas.

(George Bernard Shaw (as cited in www.quotes.net/quote/39718))

Sharing ideas and expertise is also an important element of twenty-first century pedagogy, which seeks to develop skills in pupils that equip them for a world in which most jobs require higher-order skills. The World Economic Forum (Soffel, 2016) has identified the ten top skills required for workers in 2015 and predicted those for 2020 as shown in Table 1.1.

Table 1.1 The top ten skills required for workers in 2015 and predicted for 2020

2015	2020
1. Complex problem solving	1. Complex problem solving
2. Critical thinking	2. Coordinating with others
3. Creativity	3. People management
4. People management	4. Critical thinking
5. Coordinating with others	5. Negotiation
6. Emotional intelligence	6. Quality control
7. Judgement and decision making	7. Service orientation
8. Service orientation	8. Judgement and decision making
9. Negotiation	9. Active listening
10. Cognitive flexibility	10. Creativity

Chapter 7 of this book discusses ways that coteaching supports pedagogy in twenty-first century classrooms.

This book provides a concise yet comprehensive guide to coteaching for teacher educators, ISTs and PSTs. Using research evidence, it illustrates how coteaching increases PST confidence during school experience, and as new teachers. It also shows coteaching as embedded professional development, which is heralded by OECD (2015) as the most effective form of teacher continuing professional development (CPD), and demonstrates how coteaching contributes to bridging the well-criticised gap between theory and practice in teaching.

Chapter 1 introduces coteaching in three main sections, describing the nature of coteaching, how it 'looks' in the classroom and comparing it with other forms of collaborative teaching.

The nature of coteaching

Coteaching Is an innovation in teacher education programmes in which PSTs and ISTs plan, teach and evaluate a short series of lessons together; it is facilitated by teacher educators. It has been introduced in teacher education programmes to improve PST confidence and enjoyment of teaching by providing structured support in the classroom during school experience.

Coteaching involves two or more teachers planning, teaching and evaluating lessons together, sharing responsibility for meeting the learning needs of pupils and, at the same time, learning from each other. It is a pedagogical model, which has developed simultaneously in different parts of the world to address some common challenges, for example:

> » PST anxiety during teaching experiences;
>
> » the gap between theory and practice experienced by PSTs and ISTs;
>
> » ineffective pupil learning as a consequence of inadequate PST practice;
>
> » pupil disaffection;
>
> » mainstreaming pupils with special needs;
>
> » the difficulty of preparing teachers as reflective practitioners.

The essence of coteaching is sharing expertise; it values the knowledge, qualities and experience that both coteachers bring to the process. Coteaching promotes more equal roles in the classroom by supporting a less hierarchical model of teaching. Such a collaborative model gives coteaching a structure to develop teacher reflection on theory, praxis and practice. It also exemplifies co-operative and collaborative practice which learners can emulate.

The development of coteaching in teacher education

I start this section with a case study of how coteaching developed in Northern Ireland.

My work on coteaching began at a meeting 15 years ago with a teacher educator colleague and a school principal, at which we were discussing ways to enhance the development of science teaching in her primary school. The principal suggested that our science PSTs (BEd undergraduates) might work on science teaching with her own teachers – she said that both might develop more confidence – in science teaching and in teaching per se. What a powerful idea! In those early days, we called it team teaching and developed a proposal for funding, based on science students (PSTs) in primary schools (SSIPS). The SSIPS project attracted significant funding, on the proviso that we carried out the work in a minimum of 25 schools. This was a daunting prospect, as we had not done any research and development work of this nature before. We enlisted help from a group of school principals to advise us about introducing this form of coteaching in their schools and, most importantly, what problems could arise without careful planning. Stepping carefully forward, we spent a further day with the school principals, ISTs and PSTs from the 25 coteaching schools in which we carried out a series of activities planned by principals and the research team, to prepare for this new way of teaching a few lessons. At the end of the day everyone signed up to introducing coteaching in the schools, and we took it from there.

This early work provided the foundations for coteaching in the UK (Northern Ireland), and can be found in Murphy and Beggs (2006) and Carlisle (2008). On presenting our findings in the USA, we met colleagues who were working on a very similar model, which they called coteaching. Coteaching (without the hyphen) is distinguished from the hyphenated term 'co-teaching' (used primarily in special education), team teaching, co-operative teaching and collaborative teaching. Coteaching is the only one of these approaches that requires a commitment to coplanning, copractice and coreflection; it serves as a methodology for preparing teachers and a pedagogy for improving teaching, and is based on a sociocultural theoretical framework. The aims of coteaching include:

> » reducing the theory–practice gap in teacher education;
>
> » improving reflective practice in the classroom;
>
> » developing teachers' pedagogical content knowledge (PCK).

Our work progressed as coteaching, in an international collaboration between the UK, Ireland, and other European countries, USA, Canada, Australia and Asia.

Even in the earliest coteaching research projects, we came across several examples of reflective comments from both ISTs and PSTs on different ways that coteaching had developed their teaching. The following example describes how a primary school coteacher critiques her own practice when observing her coteaching PST as she interacts with pupils.

*One of the main things that I gained was that you could **sit back and watch your children responding to somebody teaching them** … You could see sometimes that there were **children in the classroom continually getting the attention from the students** [PSTs], because they were the loudest, always coming up with answers, always being funny. They were getting the attention and there were children who were being completely ignored… because they were quiet and sitting not making a sound but not showing any interest. **It made me aware that I'm probably doing that in my teaching** … To be able to see someone else teaching because you never do that…*

The comment that follows from a PST describes the difference between the experience of the more traditional 'teaching practice' and that of coteaching.

*You come into school on 'teaching practice' and maybe you are sitting there observing the class when the teacher is taking the lesson. You see things and you want to say something or do something in response to whatever has gone on and you can't really. But with the coteaching you were really into it, you were **more of a legitimate participant in***

things, *you were* **watching and learning from the teacher as you were teaching,** *so if there was something you thought could go differently* **you could just intervene and that would be OK.**

Our initial model of coteaching in a primary science context, which illustrates the sharing of expertise, is illustrated in Figure 1.1.

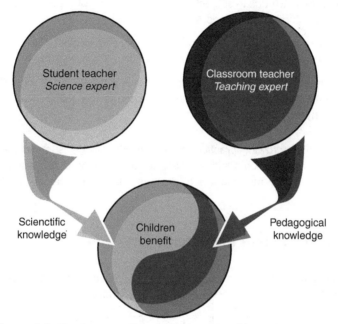

Figure 1.1 Sharing expertise model for coteaching primary science

The benefits for pupils from coteaching have been highlighted in large research projects, and include significantly higher attainment scores in mathematics and reading on national tests in the USA (Bacharach, Heck and Dahlberg, 2010b) and significant improvement of attitudes to science lessons and problem solving (Murphy and Beggs, 2010).

Coteaching is now an established practice in teacher education globally, most widespread in the USA. Research evidence shows multiple benefits for all participants in coteaching, which are considered in more depth in Chapter 6, and include:

> » PSTs involved in coteaching are typically more confident and agentic (proactive, self-reflective), attain higher school experience grades, enjoy teaching more and exhibit better decision making (eg Scantlebury, Gallo-Fox and Wassell, 2008; Murphy, McCullagh and Doherty, 2014);

> » coteaching ISTs are still involved in teaching their own classes during the coteaching lessons; no longer spectators in the room;

» coteaching presents ISTs with excellent, embedded professional development opportunities (eg Nilsson, 2015; OECD, 2016);

» coteachers can exploit opportunities to experiment with new instructional strategies, monitor pupils more closely and gain from the teaching conversations which take place at all stages of coteaching (eg Gallo-Fox, 2010);

» improved pupil learning (as measured by scores in externally administered tests), improved attitudes to subject learning and to school in general (Bacharach et al, 2010b; Murphy and Beggs, 2010);

» teacher educators get the opportunity to teach alongside PSTs and ISTs, and to learn more about putting theory into practice (Carlisle, 2008);

» significant whole-school impact of coteaching in terms of culture, teacher morale and increased enthusiasm to engage in outside initiatives (Kerin and Murphy, 2015).

Coteaching is now a growing practice in several other fields, such as between school librarians and teachers, parents and teachers, teacher education colleagues with different specialisms, professional musicians and teachers, teacher educators and teachers, and two teachers.

Coteaching in the classroom

Coteaching comprises three phases: coplanning, copractice and coreflection, which are interdependent. Each phase is discussed in depth in Chapter 4.

1. Coplanning is an essential aspect of coteaching. It provides opportunities for joint responsibility for the lesson and facilitates coteachers in clarifying their individual roles in relation to the particular lesson. In coplanning, coteachers plan 'ideal' lessons that aim to enhance learning for all pupils, instead of focusing on resources and their use.

2. Copractice describes coteachers' roles in the classroom. During the lesson, it would be rare for both teachers to be 'on the stage' throughout. More commonly, they move between roles during the lesson, depending on the activity. When copractice is fully attained, the praxis of teaching (teaching as consciously linking theory and practice) is mutual and coteachers are able to anticipate each other's moves.

3. Coreflection is required to guide coplanning for the next session using lessons learned. Coteachers reflect in the 'ideal plane', whereby they seek tools (perhaps advice from colleagues, books, online references, etc) and model solutions to episodes in the lesson that were not as successful as they had hoped (see Chapter 4 and Appendix 4 for more details on coreflection).

It is when coteachers are copractising in the classroom that we get the best illustration of how coteaching works. During a single lesson, there are many different ways that coteachers work together (see Figure 1.2).

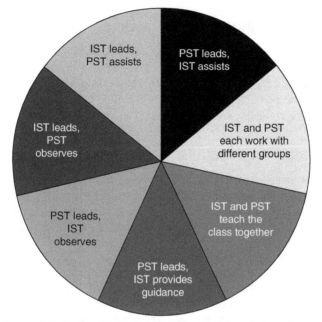

Figure 1.2 Some different forms of coteaching during a lesson

One coteacher leading, the other assisting

Depending on the content and/or activity, it is best that one coteacher leads, for example, by giving a set of instructions and watching the pupils, while the other is using props or illustrations to assist. This arrangement suits a range of activities which require more than one set of hands to set up a more ideal learning environment.

One coteacher leading, the other observing

This approach is used when one coteacher might be trying something new or unfamiliar and the other watches the pupils to assess how it is working out. Observation during coteaching focuses on the pupils, rather than on the teachers. It is frequently employed early in coteaching when the PST might value the IST's advice. But as coteachers become more comfortable with each other, they both ask to be observed trying out new resources or teaching methods.

Coteachers working separately with small groups

During practical activities, it is often valuable for teachers to pay attention to small groups. Having two teachers doubles this opportunity!

One coteacher leading, the other guiding

This approach provides an excellent example for pupils, when they observe the IST taking verbal guidance from the PST and vice versa, as they try something new. Pupils see good collaboration in action as the coteachers model taking and using advice – and their responses when the outcome is not as planned. For coteachers, this approach enables them to develop their teaching while 'in the act'.

Coteachers teaching together

This approach is most successful when coteachers have got used to working together. A huge advantage of this method is that pupils can benefit from two perspectives at the same time, and thus experience learning more fully. Coteachers plan lessons that are sufficiently flexible to enable each to 'step forward' or 'step back' accordingly to maximise the contribution of their expertise to the learning environment.

You can see video clips of these different forms of copractice online at: www.pstt.org.uk/ext/cpd/coteaching/8.html. The blend of coplanning, copractice and coreflection is one feature that distinguishes coteaching from many other collaborative forms of teaching. The next section compares coteaching with some other popular collaborative approaches.

Comparing coteaching and other collaborative teaching models

Perhaps the major difference between coteaching and other forms of collaborative teaching is that coteaching is specifically developed for improving the school experience element of initial teacher education. Most other forms of collaboration in teaching involve ISTs working together in the classroom, sometimes with non-teaching specialists.

My own experience of teaching in a wide variety of contexts suggests that there is no single 'one-size-fits-all' approach for classroom collaboration. Table 1.2 shows some forms of collaboration which are frequently compared with coteaching.

Table 1.2 Different forms of collaboration in teaching

	Typical context	Rationale	Share of responsibilities during instruction
Team teaching	ISTs and specialists	Providing expert knowledge and practice	Teachers commonly teach different pupils
Lesson study	ISTs	Developing a scholarship of teaching and improving pedagogic practice	One teacher instructs; others observe
Co-teaching	Inclusion classes (mostly in the USA)	Optimising learning for special needs pupils in inclusion classes	Usually the inclusion teacher works with special needs pupils
Coteaching	Initial teacher education	Developing PST confidence and expertise; opportunity for 'on-site' IST professional development	Coteachers share responsibility for all aspects of instruction via coplanning, copractice and coreflection.

Team teaching

The term team teaching embraces most forms of collaborative teaching (O'Murchu, 2011). The most common forms of team teaching are as follows.

» Traditional team teaching: both teachers actively share the instruction of content and skills, both teachers accept equal responsibility for all pupils and both teachers are actively involved throughout the class.

» Lead and support teaching: one teacher leads the lesson assuming responsibility for teaching the content, the other teacher provides support and follow-up activities.

» Parallel instruction: the class is divided into two groups and each teacher delivers the same content and skills. Both teachers are performing the same tasks in parallel fashion.

» Differentiated split-class team teaching: the class is divided into two groups according to a specified learning need. Each group is provided with activities to meet that specified need.

These models of team teaching illustrate different levels of collaboration, with the traditional team teaching model being that showing the highest level. Coteaching is distinguished from traditional team teaching by its even higher level of collaboration as coteachers plan, teach and reflect on lessons together, with the dual aims of improving learning for the pupils and also to help develop each other's teaching repertoire.

Lesson study

Lesson study is a collaborative practice where teachers come together as a group to plan, teach, observe and reflect on a particular research lesson (see Lewis et al (2006) for a good introduction). The research lesson is one that is planned collaboratively, focusing on professional dialogue between teachers. The resulting research lesson therefore incorporates teachers' shared ideas and experiences of different approaches, resources and content for a particular subject topic. It is planned in relation to goals set for pupil learning. Usually one of the teachers delivers the research lesson while the others observe and collect data on pupil learning and development. The data are used to reflect on the lesson more broadly, after which revisions are made and the refined research lesson is taught to a new group of pupils.

Lesson study and coteaching both rely on sharing expertise, although lesson study typically involves several teachers, whereas in coteaching there are rarely more than two or three involved. Another difference between the two approaches is that in lesson study only one of the teachers is responsible for instruction during a single lesson, while coteachers share instruction as well as planning and reflecting. Lesson study is used less commonly than coteaching in initial teacher education programmes.

Co-teaching and coteaching

Co-teaching (with the hyphen) is commonly used in classes with special needs pupils and involves a general co-teacher and a co-teacher who is specifically trained in teaching pupils with special needs (often called an inclusion teacher). This model is used widely in the USA (Martin, 2009a). The inclusion teacher also implements the individual education plan (IEP) for pupils with special needs. Both educators on the co-teaching team are responsible for differentiating the instructional planning and delivery, assessment of pupil achievement, and classroom management.

There are several collaborative teaching approaches for working together in co-teaching partnerships to differentiate instruction, which are similar to those described above for team teaching, but which focus on providing specialised instruction for the special needs pupils.

Co-teaching and coteaching are similar in that coteachers share expertise. One of the key differences is in the context, which is mostly initial teacher education for coteaching and special education for co-teaching. In addition, co-teachers focus mainly on either mainstream or special needs pupils, whereas coteachers share equal responsibility for all pupils. The main difference is the dual emphasis of coteaching on both the pupils' learning and on their mutual professional development.

This section has compared coteaching with other popular collaborative teaching approaches. A key characteristic of coteaching that distinguishes it from other collaborative approaches and which makes it important in initial teacher education is the joint emphasis on coteachers improving the learning of all pupils in the class and learning from each other to improve their own repertoire to develop the ability to create new practices in their teaching.

IN A **NUTSHELL**

This chapter sets out a warrant for coteaching in teacher education and describes what it is, what it looks like and how it differs from other collaborative models of teaching.

Key features of coteaching are that:

» coteachers share knowledge and expertise, work to their individual strengths as appropriate, support each other in developing their practice to a higher level, and evaluate their progress after each lesson to improve subsequent coplanning and copractice;

» coteaching improves both PST and IST teaching practice, and PST confidence in classroom teaching increases significantly as a result of coteaching;

» coteaching can take many forms during a single lesson; it is not always the case that both coteachers are instructing simultaneously;

» good coteaching happens when coteachers are inducted into the process;

» coteaching is different from many other models of collaborative teaching, in that it has a joint focus both on pupil learning and on coteachers learning from each other *while they are teaching*.

The following quote from a PST serves as an illustration of how two coteachers decided to deal with 'correcting' each other in front of the pupils!

If I was speaking and then the teacher spoke or if it was my lesson to lead or my teacher was leading and she was saying something that wasn't completely correct, or wasn't scientifically correct, she would have said 'now if I say something wrong jump in and correct me'. She always made a joke 'see teachers make mistakes too' and that made the whole making mistakes OK for all the children. And if I did the same and did something silly, or forget the word you are trying to use or something, and [teacher name] had stepped in, it was all 'teachers make mistakes too'. And I found that you felt more comfortable and you didn't feel, I didn't feel, like a guest in her room. By halfway through teaching practice you sort of felt like you belonged there and you had the same right to step into her lesson as she had stepping into your lesson.

REFLECTIONS ON **CRITICAL ISSUES**

- *Coteaching is an innovative pedagogy in which PSTs and ISTs work together in all aspects of planning, teaching and evaluating for a short series of lessons during school experience. It serves as a bridge to link observation and solo teaching. Research has shown multiple benefits for PSTs and ISTs arising from coteaching, including increased confidence, a greater repertoire of teaching approaches and in-situ professional development.*

- *Coteaching does not always involve both teachers at the front of the class. During a lesson, coteachers carry out many different approaches they have coplanned to enhance the learning environment most effectively. For example, one might be introducing and demonstrating an activity as the other is assisting, they might then work separately with different groups during the activity, and might end the lesson together in an all-class plenary.*

- *Coteaching is different from other forms of collaborative teaching, principally because it has a dual focus whereby coteachers strive for further mutual development of their own teaching practices in addition to improving the learning and enjoyment of pupils.*

CRITICAL **ISSUES**

- *Coteaching is grounded within solid education theoretical foundations based on the work of key theorists and practitioners.*

- *The theoretical underpinnings show how coteachers can optimise on both their pupils' and their own learning gains from coteaching.*

- *Coteaching, as with other teaching approaches, has the potential to transform learning.*

Introduction

Coteaching is based firmly on the principle of sharing expertise. But how does this happen during coplanning, copractice and coevaluation? Just asking two or more teachers to work together is not always going to lead to successful coteaching. There needs to be some kind of catalyst or spark which stimulates individual and/or collective 'aha' moments that inspire coteachers as they interact, and then to move towards developing successful coteaching partnerships. This chapter explores ideas from educational theorists and practitioners that help us to locate the essential spark which ignites the most productive social interactions. You will see that a lot of the key ideas have developed from a close reading of the works of Vygostky, whose focus on learning as individuals in social contexts inspired much of the work I have carried out with coteachers and colleagues worldwide over the past 15 years. There are three sections, which explain how learning between coteachers can be sparked, shared and developed over a series of lessons.

Section 1: Sparking learning between coteachers – the dramatic collision

Vygotsky developed a mechanism for how higher-order learning created between people is appropriated by individuals. His idea was termed 'kategoria', a term used chiefly in Russian theatre and film, meaning a dramatic collision, which describes an inner tension causing a change in interest, motive or emotion and leads to change in behaviour. For Vygotsky, a dramatic collision must be experienced for the development of higher-order thinking, such as reflection. He argued that all that is taught is not always learned and does not necessarily lead to the development of higher mental functions (HMF), such as voluntary attention, reflection and metacognition. Thus in coteaching, we can use the idea of dramatic collision to represent the 'sparks' that occur between coteachers and their students which lead to learning.

The idea of dramatic collision in learning is helpful in that in any learning situation, only certain aspects lead to the creation of an 'aha' moment of understanding, or the need to find out more about something. Dramatic collisions in coteaching can spark very effective learning, from interactions that cause both positive and negative emotions. For example, a classroom teacher reflecting on her own practice while observing the pre-service coteacher:

… there was sometimes children in the classroom continually getting the attention from the student teacher because they were the loudest who were always coming up with answers, always being funny… and there were other children who were being completely ignored… because they were quiet and sitting not making a sound but not showing any interest. It made me aware that I'm probably doing that in my own teaching …

(Roth and Tobin, 2006)

Much deep learning comes from dramatic collisions that lead to self-examination. A further example of learning from self-examination as a result of dramatic collision comes from the reflections of Carambo:

Difference [between coteachers] achieves this [self-examination and change] because it does not allow for the reinforcement of the acceptable or the familiar, rather it provokes the examination of one's assumptions, and challenges our orthodox, habituated thoughts… the more difficult coteaching events forced me [Carambo] to reexamine my perspectives in light of those represented by my coteachers.

(Carambo and Stickney, 2009, p 435)

Experiencing some kind of dramatic collision can be the starting point for deep and sustained learning. This is contingent upon an environment which is conducive to learning during coplanning, copractice and coevaluation. Several theories and ideas attempt to explain social learning, including 'situated learning', originated by Lave (1988), which suggests that learning is unintentional and situated within authentic activity, context and culture. While some learning could well occur in this way, learning through coteaching requires more deliberation on the part of the coteachers in both their interactions with each other and with students. Bandura's (1977) social learning theory states that learning occurs via internalising or adopting another person's behaviour. This provides a suitable introduction to the ideas to be developed in the next section that explores social learning in coteaching from a Vygotskian developmental perspective and adds to Bandura's theory on the roles of emotion, ideal form and reflection.

Section 2: Sharing learning – the zone of proximal development

Developing learning between coteachers requires that the learning which occurs via dramatic collisions can be harnessed so that the individual learning of each coteacher can contribute to the development of their joint enterprise in the classroom. How to share learning in coteaching can be theorised using Vygotsky's 'zone of proximal development' (ZPD). The ZPD suggests conditions required for effective coteaching and provides a set of tools that educators can apply to optimise the design and development of coteaching as an educational model for the crucial element of school experience in PST education and as professional development for ISTs.

So, what *is* the ZPD? Vygotsky characterised it as *'functions which have not yet matured but are in the process of maturing… "buds" or "flowers" of development rather than "fruits" of development'* (Vygotsky, 1978, p 86) and proposed that it represents *'the domain of transitions that are accessible by the child'* (Vygotsky, 1934/1987, p 211). Many researchers describe the ZPD as interaction that is collaboratively produced in the interaction between learner and teacher.

In this chapter, I use the ZPD from a Vygotskian cultural-historical perspective as a conceptual tool to help elaborate on interactions between individuals and their environments. In this way coteaching can be thought of as a ZPD which fosters teacher professional development.

The ZPD in coteaching

Vygotsky developed the ZPD within his cultural-historical theory, which explains the basis of social transformation via the development of HMFs from the social to the individual. His work was carried out in Russia, mostly in the Soviet era following the 1917 revolution, within a framework of social reform/transformation to develop Russia from devastation due to war, famine and plague, towards becoming a superpower. The ZPD was seen as a tool to promote development and learning.

Interpretations of the ZPD suggest it is a two-way learning process with all participants learning through interactions with each other. Both ISTs and PSTs can expand their opportunities for learning while coteaching.

Development is complex, but sometimes misrepresented as a simple, linear process. Figure 2.1 illustrates an example of how teacher change might come about via professional development:

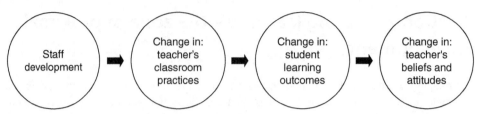

Figure 2.1 A model of the process of teacher change critiqued by Guskey (1986)

Such models, using the representation of an arrow, assume that subsequent stages necessarily follow each other, without acknowledging that many interacting conditions determine such progression. Other models acknowledge that teacher professional development is complex, but describe the complexity as existing externally, rather than incorporating it into a model. In coteaching research, we are interested in *how* development occurs. Vygotsky's ZPD comprises all the interactions required to move from one stage of development to the next. Thus the arrow (as in Figure 2.2) can be thought of as a ZPD linking successive stages of development. In this way, coteaching can be described as a ZPD in the process of teacher professional development in both PSTs and ISTs.

There are essential elements to the ZPD, without which development to the next stage will not occur at all, or only weakly. In my search of Vygotskian theory for essential elements for coteaching as a ZPD to enable aspects of professional development, I selected the following, and carried out a year-long pilot study with research colleagues and a group of 20 coteachers. We were interested in finding out which, if any, of these were valuable to coteachers in guiding their work (Murphy, McCullagh and Doherty, 2014). We assigned each of these elements to the three phases of coplanning, copractice and coevaluation. The elements ascribed to each phase are shown in Table 2.1.

Table 2.1 Elements of Vygotsky's ZPD in the three coteaching phases

Coteaching phase	Vygotskian elements
Coplanning	• Interaction between real and ideal form • Buds of development
Copractice	• Imitation • Unity of affect and intellect
Coevaluation	• Regression/recursion • Structured reflection

Interaction between real and ideal form

Vygotsky advocated the necessity from our earliest stages of development of having an ideal in mind because such an ideal provides the coteachers with motive and focus. The ideal is the perfect end-point of development which is never reached, but which we strive to attain. Yet, no development is possible without interaction between the ideal and real forms. If we don't know what we are moving towards, we'll never get there. Applying this element to coteaching involves coteachers identifying 'ideal' practice based on theories about learning and learners as they coplan lessons. When PST coteachers and IST coteachers coplan, ideas about new teaching approaches learned by PSTs from teacher educators can be 'tested' in the classroom using the experience of the IST. Here we see the opportunity of linking theory and practice closely, and the potential for the development of new theory. The ideal-real notion is akin to theory-practice. Thus, coteaching provides opportunities for coteachers to theorise and test theory, with the result that new, local theory can be produced via the sharing of expertise regarding the latest theoretical ideas and rich contextual knowledge. Teacher educators involved with coteaching can play a key role here in supporting PSTs to theorise about their practice.

Results from our pilot study showed that both PST and IST coteachers found the idea of ideal practice really useful in their coplanning, and later, in solo planning after coteaching had finished, for example:

Before I focused on resources and how they worked, whereas after coteaching I went: "okay this group didn't get this, and this is why I think they didn't get it, so this is what I'll do instead next time". It was much more detailed in terms of children's learning instead of the practical setup of the classroom.

(In-service primary teacher, interview)

Buds of development

The best learning occurs within the ZPD when the learner is at a stage, a bud or flower according to Vygotsky (1978), which is proximal (or close) to the next level of development. Good coteaching is not haphazard or spontaneous, but the result of coplanning, which requires the participation and involvement of all coteachers. Coplanning as a ZPD involves coteachers identifying 'buds' of development and supporting each other via sharing expertise and cultural tools to further develop these buds.

Imitation

Vygotsky's notion of 'imitation' is not copying but emulation (where coteachers strive to equal or excel, not merely to copy) of an activity as part of the learning process. Effective imitation within the ZPD pushes learning and development to a higher level, with successful emulation indicating the level of development of a maturing function. During copractice, Vygotskian imitation can be enacted as one coteacher emulating the practice of the other that is nearer to the ideal, thereby expanding his or her agency in relation to creating his or her new practice.

Vygotskian imitation was a valuable construct for coteachers in our pilot study, as reflected in the following comment from a PST in her reflective essay on coteaching:

...as such I seemed to move from the surface level to the more pedagogical and critical levels of reflection quicker, as I asked the questions the [coteaching partner] teacher would have asked, such as: 'where is the progression in this lesson?' 'is this particular aspect of the lesson beneficial to learning?' 'how can you overcome the common misconceptions a child will make in this lesson?' etc.

(Pre-service primary teacher)

Unity of affect and intellect

The unity of affect and intellect in Vygotsky's ZPD, that emotion and learning are interdependent, foregrounds the importance of emotion in learning. Awareness of learning occurs via emotional experience (negative as well as positive) and can be harnessed to develop better understanding of each other's needs as coteachers, so that, in turn, the collaboration can generate conditions that engage the emotions of their pupils to improve their interest and achievement.

Regression/recursion

Linked to the key role of emotion and self-awareness, a learner's behaviour as it affects learning is the realisation that learning can be difficult, and that it does not always assume a smooth upward trajectory. Regression is key to deep learning. Tharp and Gallimore (1988) proposed a four-stage model of the ZPD that addressed the development of any performance capacity based on the relationship between self-control and social control in an activity, which includes a 'recursive loop' in which learners revert to an earlier stage and progress through subsequent stages back to where they were – in effect they re-learn (see Figure 2.2).

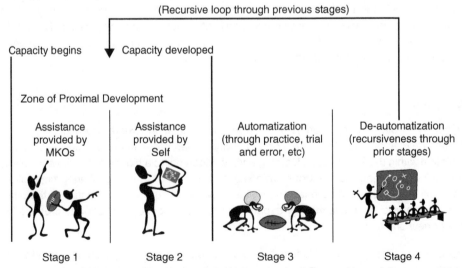

Figure 2.2 Modified version of Tharp and Gallimore's (1988) four-stage model of the ZPD based on assistance provided by more knowledgeable other(s) (MKO) (graphics added)

» In Stage 1 of Tharp and Gallimore's (1988) model, the learner relies on assistance (mostly via language) from more capable others to carry out a task.

» In Stage 2 the learner can self-assist.

» By Stage 3, the task is performed automatically.

» Stage 4 comprises the 'recursive loop' in which de-automatisation of performance leads to recursion back through the ZPD.

Examples of de-automatisation in teacher learning could be observed when a teacher is trying a new pedagogical approach, such as coteaching, or introducing new 'tools' (for example: SMARTBoards). In these situations, some 'automatic' aspects of teaching are lost, and need to be re-learned. Further learning is made up of these same regulated ZPD sequences, from other- to self-regulation, recurring over and over again for the development of current and new capacities. There is a mix of other-regulation, self-regulation, and automatised processes for each learner at any one time. Therefore, even the expert can benefit from regulation for enhancement and maintenance of performance (for example, teachers undergoing professional development). Tharp and Gallimore (1988) suggested that de-automatisation and recursion occur regularly: '*What one formerly could do, one can no longer do*' (p 187). It is frequently observed, however, that self-regulation is not sufficient to restore performance capacity after de-automatisation and so other-assistance is again required.

Other researchers have indicated the importance of regression and recursion in development, for example, the image of a tidal wave in relation to Vygotsky's work on development as a process that is progressive and regressive at the same time.

Structured reflection

During reflection, it is important for coteachers to accept that as they develop towards creating new practice, the path will not always be smooth. Consistent with Vygotsky's theory, Lampert-Shepel (1999) suggested that because human action has a dual character – ideal and real – structuring coreflection requires coteachers to explore how their practice was progressing towards the 'ideal'. Coteaching provides the potential for deep learning through coreflection by PSTs in particular, who frequently use a 'trial and error' method. We introduce coteachers to reflection 'tools' including Lampert-Shepel's (1999) model of the reflective process and an adapted version of Larrivee's (2008) tool to assess teachers' level of reflective practice (described in Chapter 4).

In the pilot study, coteachers did not refer to regression as such, but more the steady improvement of their coteaching, for example:

During the first lessons, the roles of the teacher and I in the classroom were arguably stagnant with one party often leading, observing or working with small groups with little flexibility present within these roles.

(Pre-service primary teacher, reflective essay)

However, through guided reflection, using the tools provided, coteachers considered the relationship between coteaching and reflective practice, for example:

Through coteaching I have developed my reflective practice through the levels of progression and in a variety of ways through reflection in action and reflection on action… It is evident that whilst coteaching has developed my reflective practice, the road to becoming a competent "reflective practitioner" will be long. Reflection is arguably a process, not a method, but a process which must be developed throughout a teaching career. This journey of effective reflection, facilitating lessons which site pupils' learning in the forefront has begun and it will be interesting to chart the progress and effectiveness of my reflections throughout my teaching career.

(Pre-service primary teacher, reflective essay)

Coteaching, like any new pedagogical approach, needs time to develop. The following section illustrates the theory on which we base our model of development from the earliest to later stages of coteaching.

Section 3: Developing from early days to experienced coteaching

The focus on coteaching as development is based on Vygotsky's concept of development, which does not include *'just evolutionary but also revolutionary changes, regression, gaps, zigzags, and conflicts'* (Vygotsky, 1931/1997, p 221). Such a complex, exciting, and visceral idea of development enables coteachers to remain confident, particularly in the early stages, when coteaching is not as straightforward.

The theoretical model we use for developing as coteachers is based on Vygotsky's cultural historical theory, which provides a framework for how high-level cognition develops between, and then within, individuals. Vygotsky argued that high-level thinking for a sizeable proportion of people is required for social transformation.

In coteaching we are aiming at improving learning for all participants, resulting in developing potential to transform classrooms to become more democratic, collaborative and focused on learning. For such transformation to be realised, however, Stetsenko (2008) argues that a *transformative-activist stance* needs to be adopted, which acknowledges teachers as active agents who effect change. In coteaching, the potential for transformation is increased as coteachers develop from early stages where they start as participants in the process, to the later stage where they are consciously sharing their contributions as coteachers (Murphy and Carlisle, 2008).

The model indicates progression through six stages, from coteaching as initial *participation* in the process, whereby coteachers could focus on their individual contexts. At this stage, the PST might have a more theoretical, research-based conception of classroom teaching whereas the IST's focus is initially the context of the here and now in the specific classroom. Recognising and bringing these together characterises the next stage of *active participation*, which can lead to the third, *co-operation* stage, as each is developing areas of their own pedagogical content knowledge (PCK) as described by Shulman (1986). Developing joint PCK represents the fourth, *shared co-operation* phase. By this stage coteachers will have developed the realisation that like any development, coteaching does not improve in a 'straight line' and that it takes time. This recognition sensitises each to the other and to the process, as they focus on their *contribution* to coplanning, copractice and coevaluation (fifth stage). Seeing what they can create *together* is the apogee of coteaching, as it results from a synergy between the coteachers which is greater than either could dream of producing alone. This defines the final, sixth stage of coteaching development.

In many solo-practice teaching settings, student teachers are either non-participant observers in the classroom or teaching while classroom teachers observe. This provides a situation whereby student teachers might find it difficult to fully understand the context of the decisions the classroom teachers make as the lesson unfolds; and how to apply this classroom knowledge to their own particular teaching situation. However, when coteaching, PSTs reported that participation improved their knowledge and confidence in teaching science and made them think more about how they could deal practically with certain aspects of science and technology and come up with new ideas which were not inhibited by the constraints of solo teaching practice. For Stetsenko (2008, p 479) this represents the emphasis of human action on development, '*the only access people have to reality is through active engagement with and participation in it rather than merely being in the world*'. The comment that follows illustrates the different experience of coteaching compared to solo teaching.

When you are out on teaching practice you are relying very much on schemes that were there and you didn't really have the confidence to just go and try practical things. There (coteaching placement) you were able to experiment with different things that you maybe wouldn't have tried in teaching practice on your own in case it didn't go right.

(Female BEd primary student, Year 4, Murphy and Carlisle (2008))

The comment from the student teacher also relates directly to the premise of development through active engagement. It was not just through being in the social context of the classroom, but through actively engaging in the lesson *with another teacher,* that the PST was able to most effectively learn about teaching. Coteaching therefore provides expanded opportunities for transformative action in learning and development through *shared* contribution, collective responsibility, expanded agency and the active promotion of each other's agency, and co-development.

IN A **NUTSHELL**

The theoretical basis for coteaching described in this chapter engages the three phases of coteaching (coplanning, copractice and coevaluation) within a ZPD, which also includes recursion to promote the constant evaluation of practice and experimentation towards improvement. It foregrounds the importance of emotional engagement at all stages, particularly at the start. Coplanning, copractice and coevaluation require coteachers to:

» share knowledge and expertise;

» work to individual strengths as appropriate;

» support each other in developing their practice to a higher level;

» evaluate their progress after each lesson such that future coplanning and copractice is improved.

The essential elements of the theoretical basis promote a joint focus on self and mutual learning at all stages of coteaching, resulting in constant examination and experimentation to enhance learning and teaching. It also sets out conditions of Vygotsky's ZPD which can lead to effective coplanning, copractice and coevaluation, thus indicating how to create a ZPD for effective coteaching, and provides a theoretical basis for a model of developing as an effective coteacher. An ideal coteaching scenario is illustrated nicely by an IST:

My teacher candidate and I 'share a brain'. It has been an awesome experience.
(Bacharach et al, 2010b, p 50)

REFLECTIONS ON **CRITICAL ISSUES**

* *Coteaching is different from other forms of team teaching in its emphasis on coteachers' mutual development of each other's practice, as well as on improving enjoyment and attainment in pupil learning. As with other collaborations, such as lesson study, coteaching is based on strong foundations in educational theory, and its practice is based on solid educational principles.*

* *Coteaching will be most successful when it is nurtured by coteachers themselves, as well as through guidance from teacher educators.*

* *Coteaching, when successful, can transform learning.*

CRITICAL ISSUES

- *How does coteaching work in different settings, for example, early years, primary and post-primary and special school classrooms?*

- *What is the effect of introducing coteaching into pre-service education programmes?*

- *Frequently asked questions (FAQs) about coteaching.*

Introduction

Coteaching in initial teacher education (ITE) has been introduced over the past 15 years or so to enhance the school experience of all involved in early childhood, primary, post-primary and special schools. Coteaching also offers opportunities for on-site PST learning and teacher professional development. The three interdependent elements of coteaching, which are common to coteaching in all settings, are coplanning, copractice and coreflection, as illustrated in Figure 3.1.

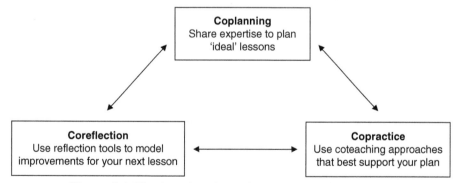

Figure 3.1 The three interdependent elements of coteaching

Other common aspects to coteaching in all contexts are the sharing of expertise and mutual respect. This chapter looks firstly at coteaching in different school settings, and then considers coteaching in ITE. The final section deals with preparing for introducing and implementing coteaching as an integral part of school experience in ITE programmes. This section includes both school experiences and research evidence to maximise the benefits which can be accrued from coteaching by all participants.

Coteaching in different school settings

This section briefly outlines models of coteaching in different school settings. For instance, in early childhood, primary schools, and some special schools, PSTs typically teach one teacher's pupils, whereas in post-primary and special schools with specialist subject teachers, it is likely that each PST can be teaching the classes of several different teachers. Models of coteaching need to be adapted to the specific school context and to accommodate solo teaching for PSTs alongside coteaching. There are some institutions that employ coteaching throughout school experience (mostly in the USA) but European models include solo teaching alongside coteaching, enabling PSTs to carry out independent practice alongside the supported cotaught lessons. PSTs are assessed only on solo teaching to ensure that maximum benefits of coteaching are not restricted by assessment of PSTs during cotaught lessons. In addition, there is a danger that assessment of coteaching could disturb ISTs, who may feel that they are also being assessed. Table 3.1 shows a variety of models that have been employed by different school/higher education institution (HEI) partnerships.

Table 3.1 A variety of coteaching models for different school settings

Coteaching models during school experience in different school settings	
Early years and primary schools	1. One PST coteaches with one teacher and one class only in a specific subject area, solo teaching in other subject areas. 2. One PST coteaches with one teacher in all subject areas for an allotted time period (say half a day per week) during school experience and solo teaches the rest of the time. 3. Two PSTs coteach with each other and the same teacher in one class and one subject area, and solo teach in the same class in other subject areas. 4. Two PSTs coteach with each other and the same teacher in one class for an allotted time (say half a day per week) and solo teach in the same class the rest of the time. 5. An entire cohort of subject specialist PSTs (typically between 10 and 12 PSTs) coteach their subject with different teachers, with solo teaching in other subjects.
Post-primary schools	1. One PST coteaches with one of the teachers and a specific pupil group, solo teaching in all other lessons in the school. 2. One PST coteaches different classes with the same teacher and solo teaches with the other teachers. 3. Two PSTs in the same class coteach with one teacher and one specific pupil group, and solo teach in the rest of their allocated lessons. 4. An entire cohort of subject specialist PSTs each coteach with one or more specific teachers, but the group of coteachers works as a community of practice, and adapt this model accordingly.
Special schools	Typically, coteaching models in special schools are negotiated by each school/HEI partnership to suit the school's context. More variation in coteaching practices in special schools exists than in most mainstream schools.

The models described in Table 3.1 do not represent all coteaching in schools. Research on coteaching describes additional models, for example, two ISTs coteaching primary science (Roth, 1998), coteaching between the university tutor and a PST (Roth and Boyd, 1999) and coteaching between parents and teachers (Willis and Ritchie, 2010). For the purposes of this text, however, the focus is on PST-IST coteaching during school experience. In my experience, it is frequently the case that standard coteaching models are adapted to suit specific contexts. For example, in some primary schools, coteaching partners who initially cotaught one subject only have extended the coteaching to other subject areas to support interdisciplinary project work. One of our current post-primary level schools requested the PST to coteach scientific inquiry with teachers who were not initially ascribed a coteaching role, and had not therefore attended coteaching induction sessions. This informal arrangement appears to be working well, probably since the request came from the school, and helped by support of the IST coteacher who had attended induction. The next two sections deal specifically with coteaching in ITE, the first giving an overview of the research and experience to date, and the final section of this chapter provides a 'how to' guide to prepare for coteaching in ITE programmes.

Coteaching in ITE

The majority of coteaching research I am currently involved in is coteaching science, and music, by ISTs and PSTs in primary and post-primary schools. The Teaching Council of Ireland is supportive of coteaching in ITE (Teaching Council, 2013) and is currently monitoring a three-year introduction of coteaching in undergraduate and postgraduate music education. Less formally, coteaching is being introduced into ITE programmes in several Irish HEIs, as well as in Northern Ireland.

Early research on coteaching in ITE was reported in Canada, USA, Australia and the UK (specifically in Northern Ireland) from the end of the twentieth to the start of the twenty-first centuries. Roth, Masciotra and Boyd (1999) introduced a model of coteaching in which the PST worked 'at the elbow' of the more experienced IST. Teaching and learning benefits accrued by the IST in these early explorations of the process resulted in coteaching developing as a more two-way exchange of expertise than a unidirectional mentoring model (Roth and Tobin, 2001).

Mutual development of teaching skills through coteaching

Coteaching has been shown to improve questioning skills of PSTs and ISTs. In a study of coteaching by Tobin, Roth and Zimmerman (2001), PSTs were initially apprehensive about coteaching but one PST articulated the benefits in terms of '...*appreciating each others talents and [to] craft our individual praxis so that it best met the students'* [pupils'] *needs'* (p 947). The PST was not merely learning to teach like the experienced teacher but developing her own teaching skills, '*individual praxis*' (p 947) through coteaching. Research by Murphy and Beggs (2005) illustrated the development of a primary PST's teaching skills by way of the interactions between the IST, PST and pupils in a question and answer session during a science lesson. The IST's interventions revealed her greater knowledge of the pupils and concern with the learning of individuals. She used names more frequently than the PST, who did seem to subconsciously pick up on this and tried to use the children's names more. However, the PST did assume greater familiarity of the children with the scientific terminology and the IST intervened as appropriate to explain or prompt the PST to explain. As the coteachers worked together the PST improved how she asked the questions to pupils, which was supported by her existing science knowledge. Later in the coteaching, as the PST gained confidence, she began to help the IST with talking about science to pupils.

Coteaching has been described as being a more *'hands on experience'* (Beers, 2005, p 79) of ITE, promoting more effective development of teaching skills. Beers suggested that coteaching created a structure to apply theory into practice through learning to teach with others. She remarked:

coteaching allowed the co-participants to witness the unconscious acts of teaching and then more meaningfully reflect on the shared experience.

(Beers, 2005, p 84)

Eick et al's (2003) study of coteaching in ITE also showed positive outcomes for PSTs' development of teaching skills. PSTs reported learning through modelling the IST's practice, supported by active IST involvement in lessons and critical reflection afterwards. They also developed teaching skills in terms of meeting the needs of particular pupils, including different learning styles and interests (Eick and Ware, 2005).

Development of PST confidence through coteaching

Much research has shown that coteaching helps confidence development because it makes PSTs feel less isolated, for example, Scantlebury et al (2008) reported that PSTs who participated in coteaching became part of or established learning communities to support their teaching. Gallo-Fox (2010) suggested that coteaching offers a supportive structure which opens up situations for risk-taking and experimentation for PSTs in school. A post-primary PST commented in an interview:

In coteaching you have someone right there to help you with something that you might not know, or something that happens during the class, or someone asks a question and you've already explained it three times and you don't know how else to explain it. There's somebody else there who could say, 'Okay, how about if we look at it this way?'... So I know that for me, in a coteaching classroom, I was much more willing to take risks.

(Gallo-Fox, 2010, p 123)

It was both surprising and interesting to see the impact of coteaching on the teaching confidence of a cohort of science-specialist primary PSTs in Northern Ireland, who had cotaught science for half a day per week for eight weeks (Murphy and Beggs, 2010).

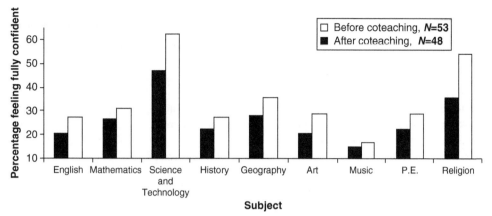

Figure 3.2 Improved PST confidence after coteaching, adapted from Carlisle (2008)

The PSTs' response to this finding was that the coteaching experience helped their confidence when they were solo teaching in all subjects apart from science. Coteaching evidences improvements in PST development of teaching skills and in their confidence to teach. In order for this to happen though, HEIs and schools need to prepare the way for introducing coteaching into their ITE programmes.

Frequently asked questions about coteaching

The following are the questions we are asked most frequently when we present our research and experience of coteaching. By 'we' I refer to coteachers (ISTs and PSTs), teacher educators, pupils and school principals. These presentations include academic conferences (national and international); presentations between coteachers during the process so that they can learn from each other's experiences; discussions about coteaching in which experienced coteachers take questions from new coteachers during induction and public presentations of coteaching at events held for education stakeholders (for example, teachers, parents, pupils, teacher educators, policy makers (local and national), teaching councils, curriculum developers, CPD organisers, and so on).

Question 1. Are PSTs assessed on coteaching?

No. Research and experience shows that PSTs are best assessed on solo teaching only. Supervision and assessment of PSTs in any context can be complex and problematic. During school experience, supervision of PSTs is commonly carried out by a combination of university teacher educators and part-time colleagues who are current or former teachers. Tensions can arise when supervisors of the same PST hold different philosophical positions on teaching and on various pedagogies, particularly when two supervisors may give conflicting advice to PSTs and value different teaching approaches.

Most models of coteaching, therefore, include solo teaching alongside coteaching during school experience. PST coteaching is never assessed, so that coteachers are free to experiment, innovate and even 'fail' temporarily as they try out new practice. Structured coreflection on each lesson serves to learn from and remodel practice to improve the learning environment. Teacher educators involved in coteaching do visit coteaching classes, but in a supportive and learning role. They typically wait on the side until invited by one of the coteachers to assist, discuss or observe. My experience in visiting cotaught lessons has involved a lot of learning. For instance, I had never taught in highly diverse classrooms before and on one occasion I needed help from a PST coteacher when pupils told me that two in the group did not understand me as they were not native speakers of English. It was very valuable for me to observe the expertise of the PST as she modelled how to include all pupils in the group – and to try it out myself. This and other similar experiences teach those of us who are in the privileged position of working with PSTs and perhaps have not taught in school for some years, that working more collaboratively in classrooms holds the potential for our own learning as well as that of our students. It also has the effect of engendering a new form of mutual respect and thus a more equal relationship between PSTs, university teacher educators and ISTs, enhancing the professionalism of all. One of the PSTs in Carlisle's (2008) study commented about a teacher educator visiting her cotaught lesson:

You don't worry about things going wrong. If you have somebody coming in to watch you, you want everything to be perfect and you put yourself under so much pressure ... and you want every child to be quiet and listen and to be doing what they are supposed to be doing but if ... somebody is coming out to join in then you are not tense and you can relax and enjoy it.

Question 2. Can coteaching risk the PST picking up poor practice?

The aim of coteaching is to provide the most effective and enjoyable learning experiences for pupils and, at the same time, to provide coteachers with the opportunity to learn from each other and to improve their own practice. In practice, as with all teaching, preparation is key to success. The stage of coplanning in coteaching is designed to avoid poor practice from either of the coteachers. The Vygotskian model, as applied to coteaching, identifies the 'ideal' as the guide in coplanning. Coteachers discuss their ideas for ideal practice regarding pupil learning in relation to each lesson and plan how they might put this into practice over the series of lessons. Being ideal, it is unlikely that perfection will be attained, but the ideal serves to point the way forward in terms of the direction of practice. The fact that joint responsibility is key in coteaching mitigates the danger of poor practice in coteaching. Of course, not all planning will work out successfully in every lesson, but such mistakes can provide excellent sources of learning towards good practice. Coteaching PSTs will bring ideas from higher education courses based on recent research to coplanning sessions. These ideas/approaches will be considered by ISTs in terms of the pupils and the learning context, and from copractice, coteachers will have the opportunity to experiment with and test approaches/ideas, sometimes creating new theory in the process.

When teachers begin working together, and share the full responsibility for planning, teaching, and reflecting on lessons, there is '*automatically a greater range of action possibilities'* and collective activity enables each individual to develop since '*any individual can now enact teaching practices not available in individual teaching*' (Roth and Tobin, 2005, p x). It is important to emphasise that sharing full responsibility applies to the overall process of coteaching, not that responsibilities should be cut in half. Rather, each coteacher should provide their individual contributions, as best serves the immediate context. In doing so, together they will create practice which moves further towards the ideal.

Question 3. What if IST and PST do not get on?

The working relationship between coteachers is undoubtedly an important factor in positive and negative experiences of coteaching. It is the case that coteaching relationships develop over time (Carlisle, 2008) but good working relations can be set up from the start with the support that induction to coteaching offers. Coteaching supports different power relationships than those assumed in a mentor-mentee context. Equal overall responsibility for cotaught classes requires that each coteacher brings their own expertise to the table in coplanning, copractice and coreflection. This does not just happen. Two major elements are needed to support successful coteaching. The first is involvement of school principals. The principal needs to be fully aware of coteaching in their school and requires good contact with the HEI. The second is coteaching induction. Both are dealt with in more detail subsequently.

A mini case study of a relationship problem in our early coteaching work involved a PST working on science teaching in a recently amalgamated primary school. Amalgamation had resulted in a certain teacher losing his post as science coordinator for the school. The principal had allocated the science PST to this IST. In an interview midway through the coteaching period, the PST spoke about her negative experience:

I hated it. I think it was because the teacher I was with was a young male teacher and he didn't take it [coteaching] seriously enough and it left me feeling very awkward because I was supposed to be writing up lessons that I was supposed to be taking and he wasn't taking it seriously enough. He thought he was doing me a favour. I tried to say to him, 'just let me get on with it, everybody else is doing plenty of work for it'. Even when I was teaching he would just take over and he was the kind of character, well, it wasn't my place to start interrupting. He just liked to run the show and I was left like a twit more times than enough. I suppose, in a different school it would have been different.

The IST in this coteaching team however, viewed coteaching as a positive experience. In the following excerpt from an interview, the IST describes the working relationship with the PST:

My student [teacher] was very knowledgeable, very helpful and very eager. She was one of the better ones, no clash of personalities. If I had asked her to do something she would have no problem doing it. I worked well with my PST and as far as I know the other teachers worked well with their PSTs. We worked it out that the start was teacher led and the PST helping and then she would take the latter half of the lesson ... I honestly can't say there were any negative points.

This example of a coteaching working relationship illustrates the importance of clear lines of communication between the PST and IST. In this scenario, the PST was not satisfied with her working relationship with her teacher and felt that the IST did not respect her contribution to coteaching. On the other hand the IST was unaware of her increasing frustrations. After this interview, the principal and coteaching leader discussed the situation and reallocated the PST to a different IST. It was this experience that changed our practice in relation to allocation of PSTs to schools to include a 'matching' process. The HEI coteaching leader of each institution discussed the PST profile with all participant coteaching schools, with the result that the principal allocated the teacher who could help achieve the best coteaching. For example, a PST might be highly confident with specific expertise in an area which the principal recognises would suit a specific teacher, or there may be a very shy PST who lacks confidence who would be allocated to a teacher who would be happy to nurture them.

Question 4. Is it extra work for ISTs?

At the start, yes – as it would be with trying any new approach. However, induction sessions are designed to give ISTs and PSTs a head start, so that coplanning, copractice and coreflection will be familiar to them once coteaching in the classroom begins. Any extra work at the start should be well outweighed by the benefits that coteaching brings to all participants. Coteaching serves as CPD for ISTs in developing their own practice by working with PSTs. In Ireland we are currently working with the Teaching Council in developing a process to *accredit* coteaching as CPD.

IN A **NUTSHELL**

This chapter describes how coteaching works in practice. It illustrates many ways that coteaching is used in different contexts, and the effects of introducing coteaching in ITE. In summary:

» coteaching can be used in many ways, and can be adapted to suit the type and location of the school, and within individual lessons to capitalise on learning opportunities, or to respond to classroom contingencies;

» the introduction of coteaching in ITE programmes has a key effect in increasing PST confidence in the classroom and can contribute to stemming the flow of early career teachers from the profession;

» introducing coteaching in ITE programmes facilitates mutual development of coteaching PSTs and ISTs;

» the answers to questions raised about coteaching indicate that PSTs are not assessed on coteaching and are not at risk of picking up bad practice;

» strategies are outlined to optimise relationships between coteachers.

REFLECTIONS ON **CRITICAL ISSUES**

- *There is no single way to coteach, as there is no single way to teach. However, this chapter sets out guidelines to optimise coteaching so that participants can accrue the multiple benefits which have been reported in the educational research literature.*

- *Coteaching in ITE programmes serves to improve relationships between PSTs and ISTs, partnerships between schools and higher education institutions, and PSTs and their teacher education tutors.*

- *Coteaching provides embedded teacher CPD for ISTs which, in some countries, is being recognised and accredited.*

CHAPTER 4 | PREPARING FOR AND IMPLEMENTING COTEACHING

CRITICAL ISSUES

- *What preparation is needed to introduce coteaching into ITE programmes?*
- *What kind of induction is needed for PSTs and ISTs?*
- *How do coteachers work together in the classroom?*

Preparation for coteaching

A core team of coteaching colleagues in the HEI and senior colleagues from the schools with which they intend to introduce coteaching into school experience for PSTs should discuss their priorities for coteaching. Schools may suggest specific areas of development which PSTs can share with the school during coteaching. Table 4.1 shows examples of priority areas for development from a variety of coteaching contexts:

Table 4.1 Some examples of specific school priorities for coteaching

	Early childhood and primary schools	Post-primary level schools
Music teaching	Whole-school approach to teaching composition for 5–12-year-olds	Implementing theory into practice
Science teaching	Using inquiry-based science in primary classes; introducing constructivist methods in science teaching; increasing activity-based science lessons; increasing outdoor science	Developing inquiry-based science; using Assessment for Learning (AfL) effectively in science lab classes; developing opportunities for field work
Addressing diversity in the classroom		Engaging immigrant Hmong children in science classes (Upadhyay and Gifford, 2010)
Developing peer observation		Coteaching between teachers in the same school as a model for improving the whole-school approach to peer observation

Table 4.1 (*cont.*)

	Early childhood and primary schools	Post-primary level schools
Use of 'learning intentions'		PSTs share the work they have carried out in college with coteaching colleagues in the classroom, who then work with other teachers in the school

Induction

Induction has been shown to be a key element to the success of coteaching. It is during induction that coteachers get opportunities to work as teams before they are in the classroom together. After a broad introduction to coteaching, in which participants consider the theory and practice of coteaching, induction will be tailored to the specific school/HEI context(s). For example, induction could include joint CPD in areas for development suggested by the school (see Table 4.2) between school (IST) and HEI (PST) coteachers, from which they can use ideas/strategies to implement together during the coteaching lessons. Coteaching induction should also involve joint activities to prepare coteachers to work together, for example, drawing up of codes of practice by coteaching teams which set out their specific ideas for working together most effectively (see Appendix 1). This sets out clearly each other's commitment to making the coteaching a positive experience for themselves and the pupils.

Additional activities during induction can help coteachers foresee situations which could cause problems, for example, repeated absence from class, and relationship issues (see Appendix 2). Early awareness and discussion of potential causes for concern is helpful in starting coteaching on a good footing.

Supported coplanning and coreflection

The final essential element to coteaching induction is supported coplanning and coreflection, in which coteachers are provided with time dedicated to starting planning lessons together, and to consider ways to reflect on planned lessons. Coplanning is essential to coteaching. It provides opportunities for joint responsibility for the lesson and facilitates coteachers in clarifying their individual roles in relation to the particular lesson. It also provides opportunities to plan 'ideal' lessons for the children, as opposed to the more pragmatic planning of lesson resources. When implementing coteaching, time for coplanning can become an issue. Thus, coplanning needs to form an integral part of coteaching induction. In advance of induction, ISTs will provide ideas for teaching content and each coteaching PST will have prepared lesson activities and other materials that could be used in the coteaching. In some cases, coteaching induction includes joint CPD, which can also be used as a basis for coplanning. Coteachers are encouraged to focus on ideal practice, whereby they plan for maximum learning and enjoyment of all pupils.

Coreflection can be aided by the use of tools, which are introduced during induction and supported by HEI coteachers throughout the duration of coteaching. Such tools include an adapted version of Larivee's levels of reflection (see Appendix 3) and an adaptation of Lampert-Shepel's model for reflecting in the ideal plane (Appendix 4). Use of these tools is described later in this chapter, under the heading *Coreflection*.

If coteaching is attempted without induction there is a danger that coteachers will fall into the traditional model of PST school experience in which PSTs and ISTs rarely work closely in planning, teaching and reflecting on lessons.

Implementing coteaching in school

Coteaching occurs in whole-class settings where two (or more) teachers share responsibility for the lesson. At different times during the lesson one of the coteachers might lead with the other providing support, or it could be that both are 'on stage' together, or both are working independently with small groups, or indeed another model which they have coplanned. The three main elements in the enactment of coteaching are coplanning, copractice and coreflection (see Chapter 3, Figure 3.1). All elements are interconnected and an essential part of the enactment of coteaching in the classroom. Effective coteaching occurs when all the elements of coteaching are fully utilised. In other words, coplanning informs coteaching, leading to coreflection, and the outcomes of coreflection inform coplanning for the next coteaching lesson.

Coplanning

Coplanning is more successful when coteachers are coordinated and flexible with their planning arrangements. Coplanning is very important for building PSTs' confidence. Coplanning also promotes solidarity between coteachers through building a collective responsibility for planning cotaught lessons.

The main constraints to coplanning are time and distance. Ways around these include the introduction of intensive coplanning sessions outside school hours in the HEI, use of email and Skype in coplanning, and in-school arrangements to provide IST cover for coplanning. It is often the case that coteachers also take time during breaks and lunchtime for extra coplanning when required. It is also the case that some coteachers may hold very different teaching philosophies and attitudes towards coteaching. Kerin and Murphy's (2015) research indicates that this constraint, if it is present, is most prevalent in the early stages of coteaching, and tends to lessen as more cotaught lessons are enacted. One example is illustrated by Gallo-Fox et al (2006):

At times I [PST] felt as though [IST] was taking charge of the coplanning sessions and also directing the way a lesson would be taught ... I'm not sure why I didn't raise my concerns with [IST]. I assume that part of my decision not to challenge her suggestions was because

I respected her as both my coteacher and as a teacher. However, my lack of voice in this situation did not allow for my opinions to be acknowledged, and decreased my share of responsibility for the lessons being planned.

(Gallo-Fox et al, 2006, paras 15 and 16)

This situation can arise when coteachers' lack of communication becomes a key inhibitor in resolving their coplanning issues. It results from a continuing commitment to the traditional one-way knowledge transfer that occurs in more traditional models of school experience (Stith, 2006). It can be avoided if addressed sufficiently well in coteaching induction (see scenarios in Appendix 2). Coplanning becomes easier and more effective after the first couple of cotaught lessons, as exemplified in these two comments from BEd PSTs in Carlisle (2008, p 136).

The relationship that I had with the teacher [coteaching IST] *developed at a steady rate. In the beginning I was aware of her concerns and apprehensions as I was in a similar situation. However, I feel that as the weeks progressed we established an excellent rapport and planned our work effectively as a team.*

(Female Year 3)

In the end we were planning science lessons with less formal structures and this gave room for manoeuvre, say, if the children came up with ideas, we were able to follow through on those ideas. It was well worth it in the end!

(Male Year 3)

Copractice

This section explores coteaching as it is practised in the classroom from early stages to more 'mature' coteaching. Coteachers tend to adopt a number of different roles within cotaught lessons, which change as they develop their coteaching in later stages. Some research (for a summary, see Carlisle, 2008) shows that during the initial cotaught lessons, PSTs often rely on guidance from the IST in the classroom, almost acting as a peripheral participant in the process. This is usually followed by the PST providing one-to-one/ group support to pupils, or leading question and answer sessions. The role of ISTs in the early weeks of the coteaching was mainly classroom management and taking the lead in teaching (Eick and Dias, 2005). ISTs also saw their role as providing support for the PST in the delivery of lesson because they had an intrinsic knowledge of the children (Kerin and Murphy, 2015). A key role of PSTs in coteaching was to bring extra resources that they have developed themselves, or obtained from the HEI for coteaching.

Tables 4.2 and 4.3 are adapted from the work of Carlisle (2008) who observed the changing roles of coteachers over ten lessons. Table 4.2 describes the first two or three lessons.

After a few lessons, the PSTs' contributions to coteaching tend to increase as they develop more confidence. Both PSTs and ISTs become more innovative in their teaching of cotaught

Table 4.2 Coteacher roles at the start of coteaching

Different coteacher roles early in coteaching	Lesson observations
IST leads and PST observes	Similar to solo teaching practice in that the IST took the lead in the lesson and the PST observed.
IST leads and PST is a peripheral participant	The IST led the lesson and the PST assisted both the IST and the pupils. The role of the PST was essentially to support the teacher in the smooth running of the lesson and look out for signs that they (the teacher or the pupils) need additional support.
IST and PST take specific parts of the lesson	IST and PST agreed on teaching specific parts of each lesson, for example, the IST delivered the introduction to the lesson and the PST took the lead in the practical part of the lesson.
IST and PST teach in small groups	Both IST and PST worked together with small groups of pupils. Most commonly observed during very practical lessons which required a higher level of pupil support.
PST leads with active support from IST	PST contributed to the science aspects of a lesson; however, the IST also contributed by guiding and supporting the PST. Useful for ISTs who were less confident teaching investigative science as it played on the strengths of the PST.

lessons. The guiding principle is to share responsibility and expertise, rather than to try and coteach in a particular way. The most effective coteaching involves PSTs and ISTs supporting each other and complementing each other's roles in the classroom. During the later weeks of coteaching, a wider variety of roles is adopted by coteachers. Table 4.3 provides a summary of additional coteacher roles in coteaching observed and reported in the later weeks of coteaching (adapted from Carlisle, 2008).

Table 4.3 Coteaching later in the placement

Teacher roles later in coteaching	Lesson observations
PST leads, IST is a peripheral participant	The PST took the lead in the lesson and the IST was in the supporting role. The PST provided the introduction to the lesson, then both coteachers were involved in any practical aspects or group work, and the PST finished up the lesson.
PST leads and IST observes	The PST took the lead in the lesson and the IST observed the main part of the lesson for coreflection purposes.

Table 4.3 (*cont.*)

Teacher roles later in coteaching	Lesson observations
Equal partnership – IST and PSTs teach lesson together	PST and IST were both equally involved in the delivery of the lesson. In many cases this involved both coteachers standing or sitting at the front of the class teaching the lesson and taking the lead seamlessly from each other.

By the fourth or fifth lesson, most coteachers become aware of both their role as supporter of the other coteacher as well as that of providing the best possible learning for the pupils. Carlisle (2008) summarises this in extracts from her interviews of coteaching PSTs and ISTs: '*she* [IST] *giving the benefit of experience, I hope to bring expert knowledge along with knowledge of new teaching methods in science*'. The IST's view of their roles mirrored the PST's 'to act as a partner to the PST … to give advice and guidance to her'. This symmetry of understanding is reflected in mature, most effective coteaching. The principle behind collective responsibility is adopting complementary roles, in that each coteacher plays to their strengths. It represents Vygotskian 'intersubjectivity' in which meaning (in this case as related to effective copractice) is shared between the coteachers and used to maximise learning and enjoyment for pupils. Later, such meaning becomes 'intrasubjective', describing how each individual coteacher captialises on the collective learning to improve on their solo practice. Carlisle (2008, p 140) cites a PST and IST reflecting on their complementary roles:

> PST: *I think it worked well, working as a team because whenever I was stuck on a question the children asked then the teacher came in and he helped me out and then there were ideas I brought in that he'd never heard of before.*

> IST: *Two adults in the room, both focused on science and complementing each other's teaching was very valuable for the children.*

Scantlebury et al's (2008) work on post-primary level coteaching in the USA revealed that coteaching was most successful when there was a mutual sense of co-respect for one another's contributions and a shared sense of co-responsibility for meeting pupils' needs. They suggested that for PSTs to share authority in classroom management, they need to 'step up' to contribute to the goals of the lesson. ISTs, on the other hand, need to 'step back' and relinquish some control to support PSTs as they move towards equal status in their contributions as coteachers.

Stepwise development of coteaching from the start to 'mature' coteaching can follow the model of social transformation described in Chapter 2, in which participation is the first stage, leading to conscious shared contribution in the final stage. A version of this development is shown in Figure 4.1, which shows how each stage can be conceptualised by coteachers.

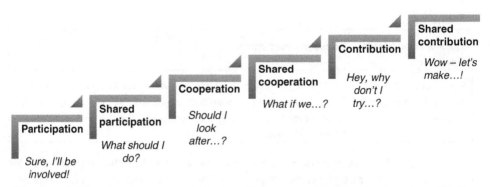

Figure 4.1 Stepwise development of coteaching from participation to shared contribution

Coreflection

The third element of enacting coteaching is coreflection. Coreflection is vital for effective coteaching. Reflection on cotaught lessons is structured, so that coteachers reflect on lessons in terms of ideal practice, as opposed to a more pragmatic focus. Coteachers consider reflection for, in and on practice respectively in terms of their coplanning, copractice and coreflection (see Figure 4.2).

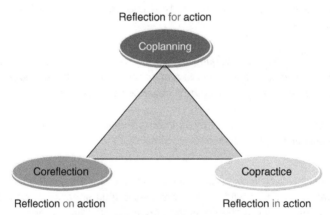

Figure 4.2 Reflection in coteaching

Three key tools are used which ensure that the level of reflection is deep, meaningful and contributes effectively to the development of teachers as reflective practitioners. The first tool is an adapted version of Larivee's (2008) levels of reflection (see Appendix 3). Coteachers can use this tool to both develop and monitor together how deeply they are reflecting on their lessons.

The second tool (see Appendix 4) is an adaptation of a model of reflection based on the work of Dewey and Vygotsky by Lampert-Shepel (1999). This tool is excellent for reflecting on addressing coteaching per se. It provides a structure to optimise how coteachers adapt their practice to develop their coteaching to be most effective for its dual purpose of improving the quality of learning for the pupils and for developing themselves as excellent coteachers and solo teachers.

The third tool is *cogenerative dialogue*, which is a specific method of generating 'solutions' together. It is used a lot in coteaching situations, but can be utilised successfully in other contexts. Cogenerative dialogue refers to the structured discussion sessions between representatives of all participants involved in a process, such as a taught lesson. The purpose of this dialogue is to generate discussion around the lesson as well as expanding the agency of each participant group or individual, which in turn will promote a collective responsibility for all aspects of the cotaught lesson. Ideally, pupils are involved in cogenerative dialogue (see Tobin, 2006) but this is not always possible. The following rules are associated with cogenerative dialogue:

>   talk should be shared among participants;
>   participants should be active listeners;
>   a mutual focus must be established from the beginning;
>   hierarchies do not apply.

Above all, cogenerative dialogue helps coteachers to develop new, innovative pedagogical practices as they reflect on their lessons.

The time available for coreflection can be limited because of the ISTs' teaching commitments and PSTs' university timetables. Coreflection *in* practice, however, can take place via 'huddles', a term used to describe in-lesson chats by coteachers to quickly reach agreement on ways to adapt the lesson as and when required. Huddles are usually informal and pragmatic, but a very important part of copractice. Pupils pick up on huddles as good practice and tend to use them in their own group work.

Coreflection, wherever and whenever it takes place, ensures that coteaching is developing in the right direction. In the early stages of coteaching, such reflection could be more structured and formalised, until it becomes an integral part of the coteaching process.

IN A **NUTSHELL**

This chapter outlines a comprehensive guide to preparing for and implementing coteaching in PST school experience. In summary:

>   induction and support throughout the coteaching period ensure that coteachers can improve the learning environment for the pupils and develop their own confidence and creative significantly in many areas of teaching
>   the processes of coplanning, copractice and coreflection can be supported by the use of some meditational tools, such as those suggested in Appendices 1–4.

REFLECTIONS ON **CRITICAL ISSUES**

- *Coteaching needs induction and support, particularly in contexts whereby either the school or PSTs have not cotaught previously.*

- *The guidance for introducing coteaching provided in this chapter is based on more than ten years of coteaching research and practice in early years, primary and post-primary school settings.*

- *Coteaching needs to develop from mere participation in the process at the start towards conscious shared contribution by coteachers in both providing an excellent learning environment for pupils and in sharing expertise to support mutual development of each other's teaching practices.*

- *Coteaching supports a high level of embedded professional development for PSTs and ISTs.*

CRITICAL **ISSUES**

- *Can coteaching support effective CPD for teachers?*
- *Is coteaching a form of CPD in itself?*
- *How can coteaching be optimised in terms of effective CPD?*

Evaluating coteaching as effective CPD

Much research in education aims at defining conditions that support effective CPD. Murphy et al (2007) underlined the importance of professional development work for teachers. They found that, in a UK-wide sample of 300 primary teachers, those who had experienced any science professional development, regardless of what type, and for how long, were significantly more confident than those who had not undertaken any professional development in science. More broadly, Kerr (2010) reviewed the international literature and summarised the following as core criteria for successful CPD:

1. active participation, including follow-up work in schools (Garet et al, 2001);

2. planned and focused upon the needs of specific teachers and pupils (PDE, 2000);

3. linking research and practice;

4. working together (teachers, universities, other agencies);

5. reflection (on good/not so good practice/process);

6. presentation of work;

7. long-term/ongoing programme (sustainability).

This section evaluates coteaching in terms of these criteria.

1. Active participation

Active participation in CPD appears to be paramount in making CPD effective, particularly when the active participation encompasses contextualised professional development with follow-up activities (Garet et al, 2001) that take place in school and are embedded in everyday work. Coteaching provides a structure in which ISTs are key active participants, who work with PSTs in the classroom to link research and practice with the aim of improving the learning environment for all. During induction programmes for coteaching, ISTs and

PSTs experience joint CPD programmes together, and implement ideas gleaned from these sessions through coteaching. Such CPD could be related to a curriculum subject, new teaching approaches, assessment, ICT or other areas of development.

2. Focus on specific teacher/student needs

Many studies suggest that focusing on the needs of specific teachers and pupils is one of the main criteria for effective CPD (for example, PDE, 2000). Coteachers' key focus is on the needs of specific and groups of pupils, and it is this principle that guides them through the cotaught lessons. At first it might feel strange to be teaching with another, but recognition that pupils can benefit from their shared expertise assists coteachers in coplanning, coteaching and coreflection. During induction, ISTs and PSTs discuss their own developmental needs, and ways they can support each other during the school experience period when they are coteaching. They reflect on this development during and following coteaching. Following induction, coteachers are encouraged to adapt materials, ideas and resources that were presented in CPD workshops, to suit both their own needs and those of the pupils. Coteachers have reported (Gallo-Fox, 2010) that the mutual support from each other supported more risk-taking in their teaching, particularly in relation to facilitating more pupil ownership of their learning (Beggs et al, 2008). They highlighted difficulties in doing this alone, outside coteaching, when trying to implement ideas from other types of CPD courses. In coteaching, further support is provided by the coteaching management team, who visit coteaching classrooms to discuss, advise and reassure coteachers about their practice. Such support is '*grounded within the context of the school*' and teachers appreciated the 'professional privacy' it afforded (Johnston et al, 2007, p 232). Teachers were more likely to discuss concerns during these visits than at seminars, where other teachers were present.

3. Linking theory, research and practice

The relationship between theory, research and practice in education has long been recognised as problematic. Bereiter (2013) characterised the learning sciences as 'an effort to overcome the much-lamented gap between research and practice in education' (p 12) and argued that neither explanatory (theoretical) knowledge nor practical (experiential) knowledge can fill the gap alone. One explanation for the gap between educational theory and the practice of teaching is the difficulty in forming an explicit 'teaching skills set' which experienced teachers develop over time. Researchers have suggested a greater link between content and pedagogy, and early experience of the application of educational theory, as ways of integrating theory and practice within initial teacher education (Ball, 2000; Dewey, 1929; Edwards and Collison, 1995). Coteaching between PSTs and ISTs can serve to lessen the gap between theory and practice.

PSTs embarking on teaching practice in schools often feel that despite knowledge of their subject matter, teaching skills and understanding of educational theories, they remain unprepared for the classroom. They experience a gap between theories of teaching (classroom management, learning and curriculum) and the practice of teaching (Roth et al, 2001). Many PSTs experience a level of *'antipathy towards most kinds of theorising'* (Kyriacou and Stephens, 1999, p 28). Initial teacher education courses need to make as explicit as possible the links between theory and practice to enable student teachers to make informed decisions concerning their classroom practice (Tomlinson, 1995).

A widely held explanation for the perceived gap between educational theory and the practice of teaching relates to the nature of the relevant knowledge (Korthangen and Kessels, 1999). When teachers are teaching in the classroom they need to respond quickly to situations in which they have little time to think. This type of action-guided professional knowledge differs from the more abstract general expert knowledge student teachers are often presented with in teacher preparation programmes.

Tobin and Roth (2006) argued that learning arising from lectures, seminars and reading about teaching cannot be considered as knowledgeable teaching. It is only through the act of teaching that student teachers acquire 'praxis-knowledge'. They suggested that if student teachers experience learning to teach by coparticipating with a more experienced practitioner there may be a lessening of the experience of the gap between talking about teaching (theory) and the actual practice of teaching (praxis) (Roth, 2001). Roth stated that by coteaching the theory–practice gap is lessened:

Teachers learn in practice and thereby acquire the modus operandi of teaching ... here theory is implicit in the practice ... so that understanding is no longer separate from judicious action in a constantly changing classroom.

(Roth, 2001, p 15)

In the context of coteaching PSTs can begin to understand better the theories taught in their university courses and how to apply them through the practice of teaching with another. Coteaching provides a structure for teacher reflection on theory, praxis and practice and has been shown to address a variety of issues in teacher education, including teacher planning, the quality of teacher pedagogical knowledge and pedagogical content knowledge, formative evaluation of student learning, and professional practice and self-efficacy. Coteaching promotes a sense of shared responsibility for teachers and increases access to social and material resources, increasing opportunities for enhancing classroom practice. Coteaching, and the subsequent need for coplanning among teachers, nullifies teachers' common practice of isolated planning. When teachers plan collaboratively and coteach those lessons, they have more opportunities to respond to the learning needs of diverse students. Coteaching between PSTs and ISTs provides a way to link theory, research and practice via the direct link between university courses and classroom practice (Siry, 2001). It facilitates a most important component of learning to teach and improving our teaching, which is the provision of opportunities to discuss actual teaching experience in the light of theoretical concepts and research findings.

4. Working together

Coteachers in many studies reflect upon the advantages of working together in coplanning, coteaching and coreflecting, both in terms of the contribution to their professional development and in terms of the students' learning and enjoyment. A typical comment from a teacher interview is:

I think it's [coteaching] *good for planning and evaluating. It's always good when two people come together and say well how do you think that went? And somebody might notice something that the other person didn't or might look on it a different way and that's, that's very useful. I think planning and evaluation particularly would be the two main benefits of the coteaching.*

(Beggs et al, 2008, p 26)

The solidarity built up between ISTs and PSTs learning together and supporting each other in this way contributes to the overall success of CPD, in that each learns by supporting the other in their joint attempt to improve learning for their pupils.

5. Co-presentation of work

Providing teachers with the opportunity to showcase their work is a common thread which runs through a lot of CPD literature. In particular, Harrison et al (2008, p 589) discussed the 'reporting on evidence' on many levels. They suggested that teachers should not only present their work, but also engage in analysis of practice, recognising good practice (own and others') and making sense of the complexities and the potential for practice to be better when teachers work together. Coming together after implementation of new practice (suggested during a professional development 'course') is one way to facilitate this type of analysis. Teachers can be given the opportunity to present their work and talk about it. In coteaching, ISTs and PSTs are facilitated to present to each other on their classroom practice. Coteaching research has shown this element to be important for both ISTs and PSTs. The following is a comment from an interview with an IST:

The presentations were very useful and I think it's always very useful to see how other people did things and even to get talking to people. Putting our heads together is usually the most beneficial of all, just even informally sometimes. The whole thing was just very good because it really made [name of the PST] *and I sit down and rethink how we were going to plan … and I think it definitely improved, very much, the whole quality of what we were teaching and how we were teaching it.*

(Kerr, 2010, p 166)

Bringing coteachers together to present their work to each other also provides space for fruitful, informal discussion, a key element of all CPD.

6. Reflection

When given the opportunity to work together in class and in preparing for and presenting their coteaching experiences, ISTs and PSTs can engage in a high level of critical reflection on themselves and their teaching. However, such high levels of reflection were observed most frequently in coteaching programmes that integrated the use of reflection tools, such as Larivee's levels of reflection and Lampert-Shepel's critical reflection cycle graphic (see Chapters 2 and 4 for more details of coreflection).

7. Long-term issues: sustainability

One of main issues with CPD is sustainability – many studies the world over suggest that CPD must be long term in order to be effective (for example, Duncombe and Armour, 2004; Garet et al, 2001; Rodrigues et al, 2003). An OECD report on embedding teacher professional development in schools concluded (OECD, 2015, p 4): *'Teachers, school leaders and policy makers should prioritise professional development activities that take place in school settings that are sustained, collaborative, and focused on problems of practice'.* Coteaching which is embedded into ITE programmes serves to provide sustainable support for ISTs and PSTs. Examples of coteaching providing sustainable long-term change include the following.

» Involvement of advisory services and curriculum developers in coteaching induction has resulted in changes to revised curriculum courses in Northern Ireland. Education and Library Board advisers incorporated many of the workshop activities used in the coteaching programme into their in-service training (CPD) for the implementation of science in the revised curriculum. They also encouraged teachers to work together as coteachers to support school implementation of the revised curriculum (Beggs et al, 2008).

» Coteaching music was introduced in the ITE programme at Trinity College Dublin (TCD) in a primary school in 2013 and in several post-primary schools in 2015. Evidence of sustainability in the primary school includes:

• Allocation of school funds for the purchase of instruments and in-service in music. There are four classes of children who now play ukulele.
• In 2016, the school received the highest rating from the Department Inspectors for teaching music.
• The school has also become involved in a science coteaching project.
• Staff and children speak fluently about music using specific vocabulary to engage in such exchanges. The staffroom evidences discussions around chord choices and the children enquire in advance of a lesson about the chords, the texture and the strumming patterns.

» In the post-primary schools, there is evidence which suggests that coteaching provides sustainable CPD, which includes:

• While many post-primary schools have developed strong partnerships with ITE providers, it is through coteaching that they describe the opportunities they have for shaping the ITE course and of the PST.
• Coteaching ISTs presented tutorials and workshops in TCD, which the PSTs found extremely valuable.
• Active participation from teachers during the monthly coteaching planning sessions ensured that each school contributed to the shape of the PST

school experience so that no one model of coteaching was enforced and thus ensuring that the needs of the school were met.

- Schools commented on the overall potential to reduce the theory–practice gap.
- Pupils and ISTs were exposed to musical skills beyond the remit of the IST. For example, having a percussionist as a coteacher presented opportunities which would otherwise not have been possible.
- Pupils clearly indicated that they enjoyed having more than one teacher in the classroom and in fact recommended it.

» An extract from a report submitted by coteachers of one of the post-primary schools to management after the first year of coteaching outlines some of the IST experiences:

Being part of this coteaching project enabled teachers to grow beyond our role as classroom teacher. We modelled good practice and facilitated coreflection after each class. Over the course of the term we also became teacher educators. Our investment in quality teaching was not restricted to how we taught but also in our desire to ensure that our coteachers would provide a quality education also, not only in our school, but in their future places of employment. The skills of shared leadership which we developed during the project became central to the success of the project and are now embedded in the second phase of the project.

» In places where coteaching has been practised for several years, we now have the cycle of teachers who were coteaching PSTs and are now coteaching ISTs, which embeds coteaching fully into ITE and CPD programmes.

» Coteaching is being used as a model for learning to teach across three teacher education programmes at the University of Delaware. The current research is designed to explore the development of coteaching as a model for teacher professional development.

Coteaching professional development (CoPD)

An alternative to traditional professional development courses is embedded professional development (EPD), defined as teacher learning that is grounded in day-to-day teaching practice and is designed to enhance teachers' content-specific instructional practices with the intent of improving student learning (Darling-Hammond and McLaughlin, 1995; Hirsh, 2009). This type of CPD focuses on connecting research to practice on an ongoing basis in collaboration with other professionals. It comprises formats such as action research, lesson study and professional learning communities. Teachers are required to be open to critical feedback and willing to share lesson plans, and tests, etc in order to improve their teaching and ultimately improve the educational environment for all students (Shaffer and Brown, 2015). This CPD format requires that for effective learning to take place, activities must be grounded in theoretical knowledge based in actual events, self-directed and significant to the teacher, and build upon pre-existing knowledge.

Shaffer and Brown (2015) also suggest that combining coteaching and EPD creates the coteaching professional development (CoPD) classrooms model.

CoPD can provide educators with many opportunities to improve on how they meet the academic and behavioural needs of increasingly diverse student populations. This model has been designed specifically for special education teaching in the USA, in which general education and special education teachers co-teach. Shaffer and Brown (2015) propose that CoPD allows the special education teacher to increase his/her knowledge of the content, for example, science or social studies, while building the pedagogy skills of the content area teacher. CoPD enables the participating teachers to have real learning opportunities in the classroom.

Coteaching between ISTs and PSTs in mainstream schools uses a similar model to CoPD described earlier, and indeed, could be presented as such. The coteaching professional development is shared between the IST and PST, and could provide an excellent basis for CPD which starts at the very beginning of teacher education and continues throughout the career. Many coteaching ISTs now started out as coteaching PSTs, so the cycle supports renewal for ISTs in terms of new theory and practice, each time they coteach with a new PST. The CoPD is thus a valuable form of CPD which, as long as it is credited accordingly, provides long-term, sustainable, embedded CPD which, with its emphasis on linking theory and practice, holds strong potential for classroom transformation.

Other models of coteaching as CPD are described in the literature. In one project, primary and post-primary science teachers worked with scientists to develop teachers' subject knowledge and confidence, scientists' knowledge of the school curriculum, to broaden and deepen children's experience of primary science and to develop a heightened sense of risk-taking in the primary science classroom (Bianchi and Murphy, 2014). The study illustrated an approach to primary teacher CPD that spans the course of an academic year (nine months), is facilitated and overseen by a university-based project manager with specific expertise in primary science curriculum development and involves research scientists. The model relies on two teachers working together from each primary school and for pupils' interests to be acknowledged and act as a core focus of interest. This contrasts with more typical CPD programmes, typically two- or three-day courses offered by a training organisation/institution.

Martin (2009b) developed a CPD course collaboratively with ISTs enrolled in the course – using cogenerative dialogue (see next chapter) to co-construct the content of the course, the assignments, and to negotiate all aspects of the syllabus. She collaborated with teachers in groups of three to coplan the course readings, assignments, assessment measures, and class activities, after which they cotaught the course. This coteaching arrangement allowed for a variety of roles in the class and effectively redistributed the division of labour among all the participants. Through the activities and conversations, ISTs began to recognise that many of the teaching practices that benefited their own learning as 'students' were not practices they implemented in their high school science classrooms. In this way, ISTs began to consider the ways in which their teaching practices afforded or impeded the learning of their students.

Optimising coteaching as CPD

How can we ensure that coteaching is indeed effective in developing teachers professionally? Gallimore et al (1992) suggest that what is gained from all relationships between mentor and mentee, or indeed any relationship which requires close working between two individuals, depends as much on the *nature of the activities* in which they are co-engaged as on the affective quality of the relationship. And, in turn, the nature of the activities will be determined by how such activities are arranged and managed.

Coteaching activity settings

To facilitate coteaching as CPD, we need to focus on ensuring that the coteaching set of lessons are planned and evaluated with mutual teacher development in mind as well as promoting excellent learning opportunities for the pupils. Gallimore et al (1992) suggest that we can do this simply in terms of the *who*, *what*, *when*, *where*, and *whys* of the coteachers, pupils, the lessons, time of year, everyday life in school, and the agreed aims of the coteaching experience for all participants. All of these features together comprise the reality of life and learning during coteaching. However, the surrounding social and cultural features, such as school and home conditions, beliefs and goals, also shape classroom activities. Planning for coteaching needs to take these factors into account. Kerin's work on coteaching music in primary schools (personal communication) is providing evidence that strongly held pedagogical beliefs could be critical in developing good working relationships during the early stages of coteaching. Coteachers need to be aware of, and to discuss, the merits of different approaches as they begin to work together so that they can create best practice via sharing ideas. This level of awareness between coteachers will influence classroom activities, and will be internalised by pupils. An interesting example from the USA shows how the effect of everyday activities can militate against cultural goals:

American cultural goals emphasize egalitarian ideals and universalistic moral convictions regarding sharing and fairness. But the day-to-day activity settings in which American children typically find themselves (e.g., classrooms, sports, individual homework) in fact encourage individualism, autonomy, competitiveness, self-direction, and self-regulation. In contrast, while many non-Western cultures have public overt beliefs emphasizing differences between clans, castes, religious groups, or regions, in their daily routines these children participate in cultural activities that emphasize shared functioning, co-regulation of behavior, compliance to adults and older children and that discourage exploration or private self-aggrandizement.

(Weisner, 1984, pp 351–52)

Optimising coteaching activity settings, therefore, requires intentional efforts to provide a learning environment which is sensitive and holds a commitment towards sociocultural factors in all aspects of the coplanning, copractice and coreflection. One of the first steps is to consider carefully the current *time*, *personnel*, *documentation*, *policies* and *other conditions* within which the coteaching intervention will take place, to maximise its potential. Coteaching is more likely to be sustained if its activities are meaningful to the wider community of the school. However, sometimes coteaching might involve whole new everyday routines, with new purposes, motives and resources, in which case sustainability will be dependent upon continued support from the higher education institute after the first coteaching experience has been completed.

CPD elements of coteaching

Coteaching as CPD takes into account all of the elements of activity design outlined in the previous section, and supports coteachers through a process of planning, teaching and reflecting which is aimed at creating new practice that moves further towards the 'ideal'. Ideal practice can never be attained fully due to constraints such as time, resources and other supports. But coteaching provides a professional learning community structure in which teachers can work together to achieve practice, which moves closer to what might be considered ideal learning for their pupils and for each other. Such activity settings could be planned using some of the guidelines provided by Gallimore et al (1992), such as:

> » assessing the competence of each coteacher for the task at hand;
> » sharing responsibility in all aspects of planning, teaching and reflecting;
> » jointly setting goal(s) which will motivate all participants;
> » developing the coteaching relationship from participation towards shared contribution as the cotaught lessons progress;
> » developing shared understanding (intersubjectivity) of pedagogical concepts.

These guidelines form the basis of high-level reflective planning and teaching, which is an overarching aim of teacher professional development. Working together as coteachers provides opportunities for mutual development of new teaching approaches and skills. Some of the following practices can support this process (adapted from Tharp, 1993):

> » modelling – offering behaviour for imitation;
> » feedback – the process of providing information on a performance as it compares to a standard;
> » task structuring – jointly planning to structure aspects of the lesson to provide development opportunities.

Coteaching affords the chance for teachers to change the way they teach within the context of their own classroom. They can capitalise on opportunities to observe others, be observed, get feedback, and to repeat this cycle throughout the coteaching experience. By working together, coteachers will have internalised a new set of values and purposes of teaching for the series of lessons in which they are sharing expertise.

Intersubjectivity

Intersubjectivity refers to the way that people think and experience the world in similar ways. When intersubjectivity is present, values are alike, and goals are alike, and more co-operation is possible, leading to more harmony. The intersubjective dimension of coteaching serves as a reward to coteachers, as it makes activities memorable, worthwhile and gratifying, which motivates them to enjoy working together. Intersubjectivity is developed via joint activity in a social setting in which shared word meanings, concepts, motivations, beliefs and expectations are acquired. Its development is supported by:

- » using signs and symbols – primarily of language;
- » developing a common understanding of the purposes and meanings of the activity;
- » using common cognitive strategies and problem solving.

Fostering intersubjectivity during coteaching leads to the development of close, fine-tuned, sustained relationships and forms the basis of coteaching as excellent CPD.

IN A **NUTSHELL**

Coteaching as CPD is an innovative and successful way to facilitate teachers and student teachers working together to implement new approaches which will enhance their professional development (change in approach, confidence, and awareness of agency) and increase children's interest and engagement in learning. For example:

- » Coteaching satisfies all of the conditions for effective CPD that have been outlined in international research.
- » Coteaching provides embedded (in-class) professional development, which is shown in many research studies to be highly effective CPD, since it is tailored to local conditions as well as global components, takes advantage of mutual support among teachers and makes effective links between theory and practice.
- » Embedded professional development combined with coteaching has been described as co-teaching professional development (CoPD).
- » Optimal conditions for coteaching as effective CPD include designing supportive activity settings, which are specifically aimed at developing coteachers as well as promoting excellent pupil learning, and developing shared meanings between coteachers (intersubjectivity).

REFLECTIONS ON **CRITICAL ISSUES**

In considering coteaching as CPD, it is important to emphasise the professional development for both coteachers when one is a PST. Professional development starts at the beginning of an ITE programme and continues throughout the teaching career. Coteaching supports excellent CPD for participating coteachers if care is taken to design effective activity settings for optimal teacher learning to take place. This chapter lays down foundations for ensuring that coteaching can be used for CPD. In Ireland, we are starting the process of working with the Teaching Council to get coteaching accredited as CPD. In the words of one teacher from a coteaching primary school in Dublin:

I've done lots of summer courses and with the best will in the world I have noticed that things are so hectic when I come back in September I can't say that I always implement what I have learned. With coteaching I'm learning and implementing simultaneously, so the children and I are learning at the same time. The fact that we are receiving the new material at different level is fascinating; I am consolidating my prior learning in music and the children are experiencing music first hand from musicians.

(Teacher, St. Vincent's GNS, May 2014)

CHAPTER 6 | WHAT ARE THE OUTCOMES OF COTEACHING?

CRITICAL **ISSUES**

- *Does coteaching hold potential to improve PSTs' confidence and performance in teaching?*
- *What are the outcomes of coteaching for ISTs and pupils?*
- *What are the broader outcomes of coteaching on partnerships between schools and universities, and on teacher educators themselves?*

Introduction

Coteaching has impacted positively on PSTs and ISTs, pupils and teacher educators. There have also been examples of coteaching benefits at whole–school level in primary schools and department level in post-primary schools. More systemically, a key feature of coteaching is its potential to reduce the theory–practice gap which has plagued teaching for decades (discussed in the previous chapter). Coteaching in this book has focused mostly on PST/IST coteaching teams, and to some extent, coteaching between two ISTs. There are other models of coteaching which have also shown positive outcomes, such as coteaching between ISTs and parents (Willis and Ritchie, 2010), ISTs and special needs experts (Gleason, Fennemore and Scantlebury, 2006), ISTs and members of specific communities, such as the Hmong people, coteaching immigrant pupils (Upadhyay and Gifford, 2010), between a teacher educator and an IST, and between pupils and teachers (Shultze, 2015). In all cases, one of the key outcomes of coteaching is the improvement of confidence in developing classroom practice for teachers and improved learning for pupils. This chapter will summarise some of the published coteaching outcomes and will introduce some new coteaching projects. It will focus on outcomes for PSTs, ISTs and pupils.

Coteaching outcomes for PSTs

The main outcome of coteaching for PSTs is their increased confidence in teaching as a result of coteaching with an IST. This is referred to briefly in Chapter 3 in terms of developing coteaching per se. Many PSTs report feeling like a *real teacher* when they are coteaching. Their reasons include sharing and managing resources (including human resources – the IST), mutual support and equal partnership, ownership and responsibility for teaching and classroom management. A key reason for the potential of coteaching in improving PST confidence in teaching arises from the increase in agency they experience while working alongside an IST. Agency can be defined in sociological terms as the capacity of individuals to act independently and/or to appropriate resources. PSTs that worked as coteachers with our team commented that they felt much more part of the classroom when they were coteaching, for example, being able to use the teacher's desk and sharing resources. Another frequent reported experience was feeling more 'legitimate' as a teacher in the classroom. As a consequence they acted 'taller' and became more confident than had they acted only as a 'pupil teacher' in school. Holzman (2010) applied Vygotsky's idea about children acting a 'head taller' in their play to her own work with adult learners in its practical applications to learners of all ages. Coteaching serves to expand the agency of all coteaching participants. The work of Roth and Tobin (2004) showed that in the context of coteaching, *'teachers expand one another's opportunities to act and hence their agency'* (p 170). PSTs' agency is expanded when they are coteaching with a class teacher and contributing to planning, teaching and evaluation of the lessons.

Risk-taking by PSTs can be viewed as an additional benefit of increased teacher candidate confidence. With the support of co-operating teachers, PSTs are much more willing to be risk-takers (Gallo-Fox, 2010). Initial steps towards risk-taking may include attempts to imitate best practices as modelled by co-operating teachers (Eick et al, 2003; Murphy and Beggs, 2010; Roth, 2005). PSTs describe an increased comfort level with ISTs' support during their teaching experience in school (Eick et al, 2003). Beers (2005) described her coteaching experience as knowing that her IST consistently supported her efforts and a PST in O'Conaill's (2010) study said the IST provided a *'sense of having a safety net'* (p 184). The supportive learning environment created through coteaching creates a sense of trust within the learning community and enhances the sense of collective responsibility. Carlisle (2010) proposed that the supportive environment provides teacher candidates with more tools than they would experience with solo planning, lessening the teacher candidates' fear of isolation.

Coteaching also provides opportunities for PSTs to experience teacher decision-making in action (Beers, 2005; Eick et al, 2003; Gallo-Fox, 2010; O'Conaill, 2010; Tobin and Roth, 2005) and to learn by example. Beers (2005) described her learning in action, *'It allowed me to examine his* [her IST's] *practice in the heat of the moment and incorporate some of his schema and practices into my own'* (p 79). Roth and Tobin (2002) describe a PST's success in learning to question pupils by enacting in practice with the IST who modelled exemplary questioning techniques. Coteachers find learning on the spot most beneficial, as well as having support to modify lessons in real time (Eick et al, 2003; Roth and Tobin, 2002). These professional interactions between the ISTs and PSTs are opportunities to engage in *'professional reasoning'* (O'Conaill, 2010, p 185). Often, professional reasoning and teacher decision-making are based on tacit knowledge. Coteaching provides opportunities to make ISTs' tacit knowledge explicit to PSTs (Bacharach et al, 2010b; Roth, 1998; Tobin and Roth, 2005). Coteaching also provides PSTs with exposure to planning strategies, instructional strategies, management strategies, content knowledge and assessment strategies. They are *'no longer initiated into the complex profession of teaching by being left to figure things out on their own'* (Bacharach et al, 2010b, p 46).

Research has shown that many PSTs who engage in coteaching achieve higher grades in assessments. In the USA, a coteaching study showed that over a three-year period, coteaching PSTs scored statistically higher than their peers in professional dispositions, and higher again in reflection and professional development, and in partnerships. In all other standards, coteaching PST mean scores were the same or higher, but not significantly (see Table 6.1).

Table 6.1 Teacher candidate summative assessment scores
(adapted from Bacharach, Heck and Dahlberg, 2010b)

Standard	Coteaching PSTs Mean (N=408)	Non-coteaching PSTs Mean (N=728)	p
Subject matter	3.37	3.36	0.55
Pupil learning	3.32	3.28	0.39
Diverse learners	3.09	3.09	0.95
Instructional strategies	3.31	3.29	0.68
Learning environment	3.28	3.28	0.94
Communication	3.32	3.32	0.98
Planning instruction	3.35	3.34	0.98
Assessment	3.06	3.06	0.82
Reflection and professional development	3.47	3.40	0.08
Partnerships	3.40	3.33	0.08
Professional dispositions	3.61	3.51	0.01

In another study, longitudinal analysis of teaching experience grades (see Figure 6.1) showed the percentages of A-grades from two groups of PSTs in a college in which coteaching was introduced as part of the teaching experience (for 8–10 lessons) for science PSTs, while the other PSTs carried out the traditional teaching experience without coteaching. Independent assessors who were not involved in coteaching and, in most cases, were not aware that science PSTs had been involved in any coteaching, carried out the grading procedure for science PSTs.

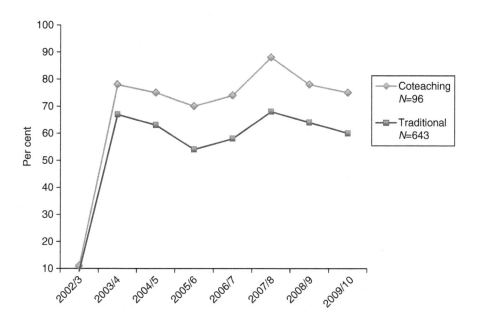

Figure 6.1 Comparative proportions of A-grades awarded for school experience teaching to PSTs who were coteaching for part of the school experience and those who completed a traditional placement. (The proportion of PSTs who achieved A-grades was routinely around 10 per cent until 2002–03 when the grade criteria were changed.)

What happens when coteaching PSTs become ISTs? One criticism applied to coteaching is that PSTs could become overdependent on the IST and thus flounder when they become 'solo' teachers. In most coteaching models, however, coteaching is carried out side by side with solo teaching during a block of school experience. Some research has followed coteaching PSTs into their first year of teaching to investigate any impact on their experience as new teachers. One of the major findings was that coteaching PSTs, on entering the profession, used collaboration as a means to support their practice. They did not report feelings of isolation and frustration felt by many first-year teachers who have not cotaught, particularly those in post-primary schools (Juck, Scantlebury and Gallo-Fox, 2010). Coteaching provides a supportive structure for PSTs, builds their confidence in teaching, and eases their transition into becoming full-time new teachers. Adoption of coteaching could contribute towards mitigating the high (45 per cent) attrition rate of teachers within their first year of teaching in the UK.

Coteaching outcomes for ISTs

Most of the benefits described in the previous section apply also to ISTs. In addition, general outcomes of coteaching for ISTs included more help with pupils with high needs, a better relationship with the PST in the classroom, professional growth through coplanning, enhanced energy for coteaching and being able to host a PST without giving up their classroom. More specifically, many ISTs reported improvement in coteaching subjects outside their expertise (for example, primary science and music) when coteaching with subject specialists. Additionally, there are reports of ISTs commenting positively on how coteaching helped them with trying out different styles of teaching, rethinking ways they teach, and justifying techniques and strategies, rather than just *'going through the motions'* (Bacharach et al, 2010b, p 50). Risk-taking by ISTs was a common feature of cotaught lessons as they enlisted the support of the PST coteacher to try something new. For example, here is a typical comment from a post-primary IST:

Something that [PST name] *talked about last year was that when you're trying something new ... it's so much easier when it's not you by yourself ... we had five of us that were coplanning, we decided to do a whole series of mini labs. Which, when you think about it; if any of us think about it. Would we ever – you know, by ourselves, would we have done everything that we ended up having to do? ... But we have – it was a support group. I mean, first of all, it was a new content [area] that most people hadn't taught, with kids who had no clue what's going on, and we were trying to put together this whole sequence of lab activities. As an individual, it would've been a totally overwhelming task, and we probably would've backed off, but together – I mean, we knew we could do it together (and we didn't give ourselves a big timeline to get it done). But with all the hands pulling together, we nailed it, got it out to the kids; and it worked so well.*

Coteaching outcomes for pupils

Pupils in cotaught classes benefit from more than one teacher, leading to increased individual attention and frequently being taught more exciting content in a more engaging way as coteachers capitalise on their mutual support to improve the learning environment. Measuring the impact of coteaching on pupils is tricky, due to the myriad of other factors which can impact on their attainment and attitudes. However, two large-scale studies show positive effects on both of these when pupils from classes which were cotaught by PSTs and ISTs are compared with those who have been taught in the more traditional way with both PST and IST solo teaching.

Bacharach et al (2010b) explored the development and implementation of a coteaching model of pre-service teaching involving formal school-university partnerships in 17 school districts over a four-year period. There were statistically significant improvements in achievement in those subjects for pupils who were cotaught in mathematics and reading classes. Some of these data are summarised in Table 6.2:

Table 6.2 K-6 (age approx. 5–12) reading and mathematics proficiency scores, measured externally via the Minnesota Comprehensive Assessment (MCA)

Reading	Cotaught (%)	Not cotaught (%)	p
2004/5	82 (N=318)	75 (N=1035)	0.007
2005/6	79 (N=484)	73 (N=1757)	0.008
2006/7	76 (N=371)	64 (N=1964)	<0.001
2007/8	81 (N=261)	61 (N=2246)	<0.001
Mathematics	Cotaught (%)	Not cotaught (%)	p
2004/5	82 (N=317)	75 (N=1032)	0.009
2005/6	69 (N=524)	64 (N=1831)	0.041
2006/7	69 (N=364)	62 (N=1984)	0.007
2007/8	75 (N=314)	60 (N=2217)	<0.001

Both primary and post-primary pupils in this study reported positive experiences of coteaching, including receiving more help from co-operating teachers, making a greater range of activities available to them, and improved pupil behaviour. The few reports of pupils' negative experiences issues included confusion from coteachers' different explanations of subject matter and, occasionally, that coteachers interrupted each other. The majority of post-primary pupils (80 per cent) indicated that they preferred coteaching to the traditional method of pupil teaching (Bacharach et al, 2007). Their study provided strong evidence of the benefits coteaching afforded for pupil learning and teacher preparation.

Murphy et al (2004) investigated attitudes of cotaught and non-cotaught children to science, six months after the coteaching intervention had taken place to see if there was any lasting impact. The chart in Figure 6.2 shows significantly more positive attitudes to science in children who were cotaught. The improved attitudes could be due to the coteaching period, but more likely it could be due to the higher confidence of the teacher, who may have been teaching more engaging science.

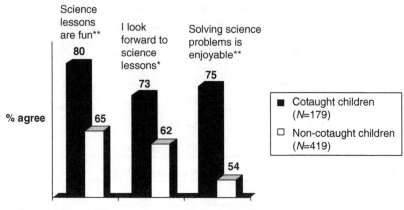

Key: significant difference at $p < 0.05^*$ or $p < 0.01^{**}$

Figure 6.2 Relative enjoyment of science lessons

Another unexpected outcome was a reduced difference between girls' and boys' preferences for different science topics in cotaught children (see Table 6.3). There was a positive shift in girls' enjoyment of physical science topics, suggesting that preference for science topics could be influenced by how they are taught. The effect of more than one coteacher (mostly female) teaching investigative science could have significantly increased girls' liking for the physical science topics.

Table 6.3 Gender preference for different science topics

Topic	Non-cotaught children (mean response)			Cotaught children (mean response)		
	Girls (N=480)	Boys (N=481)	p	Girls (N=172)	Boys (N=114)	p
	'Biology-related' topics					
Ourselves	2.79	2.67	**g	2.80	2.54	*g
Health education	2.76	2.58	**g	2.72	2.54	–
Animals	2.79	2.76	–	2.82	2.70	–
Plants	2.51	2.37	*g	2.56	2.44	–
Life cycles	2.48	2.49	–	2.56	2.19	**g
	'Chemistry-related' topics					
Materials	2.50	2.35	*g	2.52	2.44	–
Solids, liquids and gases	2.42	2.49	–	2.55	2.54	–

Table 6.3 (*cont.*)

Topic	Non-cotaught children (mean response)			Cotaught children (mean response)		
	Girls (*N*=480)	Boys (*N*=481)	*p*	Girls (*N*=172)	Boys (*N*=114)	*p*
Water cycle	2.39	2.35	–	2.37	2.46	–
Rusting	2.04	2.09	–	2.14	2.10	–
Environment	2.65	2.58	–	2.56	2.46	–
Recycling	2.61	2.52	–	2.67	2.58	–
		'Physics-related' topics				
Forces	2.30	2.53	**b	2.36	2.41	–
Electricity	2.60	2.73	*b	2.72	2.74	–
Energy	2.63	2.67	–	2.68	2.67	–
Sound	2.62	2.62	–	2.68	2.46	–
Light	2.67	2.67	–	2.60	2.54	–

Key: *b and *g is significant difference at $p < 0.05$; **b and **g is significant difference at $p < 0.01$.

Enjoyment of science was shown to be greater in older children who had been cotaught. Coteaching, therefore, seems to have a very positive effect on children's interest and enjoyment of science, and could be used to combat the reported decline in children's interest in science as they reach the more senior primary classes (9–11 years).

Broader outcomes of coteaching

Coteaching strengthens partnerships between schools and universities due to institutions working more closely together and learning from each other's professional contexts. Coteacher induction usually takes place in the university, and teacher educators visit coteaching classrooms in a supportive (non-assessment) capacity. Teacher educators are invited to join in the teaching as and when appropriate. This opportunity provides a valuable experience for those who might not have taught in diverse classrooms.

Considering the broad area of teacher education, this chapter on outcomes closes with advice from Bacharach et al (2010b, p 50) who argue that the coteaching model, which pairs ISTs and PSTs, increases academic achievement of pupils in the classroom. There has been a large uptake of ISTs hosting coteaching PSTs as they have observed the 'value added' effects of coteaching.

Teaching has become an incredibly complex and demanding profession ... We need to provide teacher candidates with tools and experiences that make the transition from student to teacher much smoother and more meaningful. By shifting from a traditional model of student [PST] teaching to a coteaching model, we no longer expect our teaching candidates to learn the complex art of teaching by leaving them alone to sink or swim. Instead, we provide them with the involvement, preparation, leadership opportunities, modeling, and coaching they need to enter their own classroom with confidence and skill.

IN A **NUTSHELL**

»   The chapter has provided strong evidence for highly positive outcomes of coteaching for PSTs, ISTs and pupils, as well as its role in reducing the gap between theory and practice.

»   There are also broader positive outcomes of coteaching institutionally for schools and universities, including embedding CPD in schools and developing more effective partnerships between schools and universities.

»   The evidence to date shows that adopting coteaching can benefit teacher education more widely and has strong potential to reduce attrition among new teachers.

REFLECTIONS ON **CRITICAL ISSUES**

This chapter has provided strong evidence for positive outcomes of coteaching for all participants. Coteaching PSTs tend to develop higher confidence and attain higher grades than those carrying out solo teaching in school experience. Cotaught pupils have been shown to achieve higher grades and have more positive attitudes than those who have not experienced coteaching. Coteaching ISTs tend to take more risks and experience more varied teaching styles when they coteach. Together with the mentoring carried out as a coteaching IST, they accomplish significant professional development. Overall, coteaching holds the potential to improve teacher education at all levels.

CRITICAL **ISSUES**

- *What is twenty-first century pedagogy?*
- *In what ways does coteaching support skills development for the twenty-first century?*
- *Does coteaching support twenty-first century conceptual learning?*

Introduction

Coteaching provides a collaborative pedagogy in teacher education, whereby coteachers share expertise to:

> » improve the learning environment for pupils; and

> » develop each other's practice.

Sharing of expertise via close collaboration is at the heart of twenty-first century pedagogy. This chapter traces the development of twenty-first century pedagogy, and shows how coteaching supports the new, postmodern approach to learning which seeks to equip pupils for life and work in a world in which economies run on creativity, innovation and collaboration.

It is no surprise that coteaching developed independently in different parts of the world late in the twentieth and early in the twenty-first century, as a way to help PSTs deal with the increasing demands required of teachers, particularly those related to effectively managing diverse classrooms. The timing coincides with the new emphasis on twenty-first century pedagogy. The current and next generation of teachers, via coteaching, can model this way of working as well as providing lessons which foster pupils' development of creativity, innovation and collaboration skills.

Twenty-first century pedagogy

The term pedagogy originates from the Greek *paidagogos*, referring to the slave who brought children to school (McLaren, 2014). Nowadays the emphasis on children (*paidia*) has become more generalised, and pedagogy is used for post-compulsory education as well as in the education of children. In this chapter pedagogy is used as a term which embraces both learning and teaching, and as a way of knowing, as well as doing.

So, what is twenty-first century pedagogy? Essentially the term describes a shift from twentieth century (modern) ways of learning and teaching to twenty-first century (postmodern) approaches. The shift is required for schools and universities to keep pace with the changes in social theory, political thought and education in the twenty-first century.

Modernism describes society from the mid-eighteenth to most of the twentieth century, which saw the development of capitalism, industrialisation, nation states and science, as well as a major expansion of European interests into the rest of the world. It was seen as a time of great 'progress'. The big ideas were that people are rational, autonomous individuals, who think and act independently of other individuals, and reason and knowledge (particularly scientific) was the route to human freedom and happiness. The big problem of these ideas is that they exclude people and groups who are marginalised from them, for example women, indigenous peoples and working-class people.

Postmodernism describes the current period in history and a set of ideas that 'go with' this period. It critiques the ideas of modernism. It is sometimes referred to as 'The Knowledge Age', an advanced form of capitalism in which knowledge and ideas are the main source of economic growth. New patterns of work and new business practices have developed, and, as a result, new kinds of workers, with new and different skills, are required. Knowledge is defined for what we can *do* with information, not for what information *is*, and is produced by 'collectivising intelligence' – that is, groups of people with complementary expertise who collaborate for specific purposes.

These changes have major implications for our education system. In order to prepare young people for successful lives in the twenty-first century, schools need to take account of the new meaning of knowledge *and* the new contexts and purposes for learning this knowledge. They need to prepare students to be able to work productively in collaboration with others. Students need to be adaptable, creative and innovative, and to be able to understand things at a 'systems' or 'big picture' level. They need to be able to think and learn for themselves, in order to help create new knowledge.

The early twenty-first century is seeing the end of traditional structures and institutions and the big, 'one-size-fits-all' stories of modern thought (Lyotard, 1984). There is no longer the idea of 'progress', that we are gradually heading along the one true pathway towards certain universal goals. Instead, there is an emphasis on multiple pathways and plurality, on diversity and difference and on the partiality of knowledge. Change is no longer seen as a linear progression, but as a '*series of networks and flows, connections and reconnections that, because they are always forming and reforming, never have time to solidify*' (NZCER online, no date). Where *modern* thought emphasises direction, order, coherence, stability, simplicity, control, autonomy and universality, *postmodern* thought emphasises fragmentation, diversity, discontinuity, contingency, pragmatism, multiplicity and connections. This has major implications for social theory, political thought and education in the twenty-first century.

Learner skills for the twenty-first century

Education is about much more than simply preparing people for work. It has other important goals: for example, developing social and citizenship skills, providing equal opportunity and building social cohesion. Education can be said to have moved from its key twentieth century role in providing basic skills and then to screen and sort students for participation in an industrial, largely localised economy, towards the twenty-first century emphasis on competences, such as self-regulation, innovation and critical thinking. These skills are summarised in Figure 7.1.

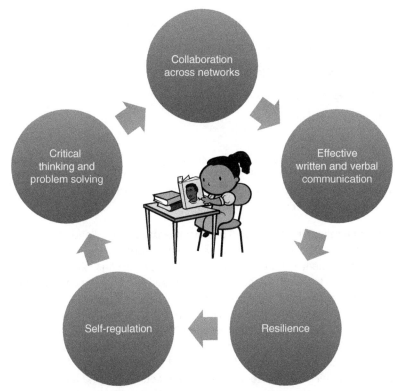

Figure 7.1 Skills of the twenty-first century learner

Coteaching as support for twenty-first century skills

The emphasis of twenty-first century learning skills on effective communication and collaboration is modelled in cotaught classrooms, in which students experience adults working closely together to enhance the learning environment. Students' comments on coteaching include some of the following, taken from various research projects.

Yes, you definitely learn more, quicker. You don't think 'I'm never going to get my question answered so I won't ask it'. You're more willing to ask the questions.

(High school student, Bacharach et al, 2010b, p 44)

An excerpt from a focus group in Carlisle's (2008, p 313) research indicated primary school children's observations of coteacher talk during a science lesson (names are pseudonyms):

Researcher (Anna): *Ok, did* [IST name] *and* [PST name] *talk to each other when they were teaching science?*

Stephen: *Yeah when* [PST name] *came in they would talk*

Sean: *They would talk when we were working in our tables making the cars*

James: [IST name] *would ask* [PST name] *questions*

Sorcha: *What we were doing?*

Mark: *They talked about the cars…*

Coteaching provides an expanded pedagogy which, by its very nature of collaborative teaching, is well suited to deliver the skills, support and pastoral care which can provide pupils with an enhanced learning environment, and improve the confidence of new teachers as they embark on a solo teaching career.

Some coteaching research has focused overtly on larger-scale collaboration work between coteaching primary schools. One such project set up a coteaching community of practice in geographically distant schools (Murphy, Carlisle and Beggs, 2007) with the aim of supporting schools in their implementation of the revised primary science curriculum (CCEA, 2007). The online community, supported by the virtual learning environment *BlackBoard*, provided an excellent support mechanism for PSTs during their school experience between each other, between PSTs and curriculum and ICT experts, and between PSTs and their university tutors. The ISTs, however, made little use of *BlackBoard*, relying on the PSTs for this aspect of coteaching, despite being trained to use *BlackBoard* themselves. Some ISTs felt that the training was inadequate. However, coteaching and the online community established strong working relationships between PSTs and ISTs and both groups reported confidence in implementing the revised curriculum. PSTs felt even more 'legitimised' (as science and ICT 'experts') and overall, the project enhanced use of ICT in primary schools. In addition, in one experiment, carried out in all 13 schools on the same day, children investigated which side of the body they used mostly for a set of different activities, such as looking (through a tube), hopping, kicking, listening, throwing, etc. The 'sidedness' data for each child doing each activity was entered into a specific area on *BlackBoard*, into which a program had been inserted to process each data-bit as it was entered. Thus each school could see their own data, as well as the overall sample from the 13 schools. The outcomes of this experiment were twofold. Firstly, ISTs were more involved with *BlackBoard* on this day than any other (they reported seeing the value of it). And secondly, the findings of this experiment were so good that they were published in a psychology journal on laterality in children (Greenwood et al, 2007), which was an unexpected bonus from the project, arising from the collaboration of ISTs, PSTs, children, researchers and psychologists.

Coteaching involving PSTs and ISTs supports students' development of all of the key skills and attitudes illustrated in Figure 7.1 by providing a key link between theory and practice in relation to twenty-first century pedagogy. Coteaching also supports the development of critical thinking skills both for the coteachers themselves as they plan, teach and reflect critically together and can give students more attention and help during problem-solving activities.

Coteaching as support for twenty-first century pedagogy

In the twenty-first century 'knowledge age', the very definition of knowledge has changed from the idea of stored information to that of knowledge as a 'form of energy', which makes things happen; as something we 'do' as opposed to that which we 'have' (Gilbert, 2005). Thus, the concepts we teach are being thought of differently. For instance, scientific concepts are no longer considered as entities, but as *tools* created in the scientific endeavour. There is a realisation now that all concepts are culture-dependent, context-bound and subject to change. This is very different from the former ideas of concepts as independent of culture, universal and permanent.

A coteaching pedagogy provides teachers with different ideas about content and how to teach it, ensuring that students are exposed to the more fluid nature of knowledge as presented by two different teachers. A comment from a coteaching PST illustrates this phenomenon:

Reflecting on the lessons we took with the children has made me realise how much they actually learned during the coteaching experience. The children were able to learn that different teachers have different opinions about subjects and coteaching gave the children the opportunity to discover this...

(Carlisle, 2008, p 196)

Twenty-first century pedagogy requires approaches that embrace the provision of appropriate *contexts* for student learning, for example, collaborative learning and application of concepts, as opposed to the learning of facts.

Twenty-first century approach to conceptual learning and its assessment

Conceptual learning in the twenty-first century model is considered as developmental and long term with regression, zigzags and gaps, not as a progressive, linear model. Coteaching allows for more attention to be given to students as they grapple with problems and difficult ideas. One of the most important features of twenty-first century learning is the focus on dialogue in learning. Assessment of twenty-first century learning comprises examining *how well students 'use' concepts*, rather than verbalising them. The coteaching approach holds potential for teachers to work with pupils as collaborators in using concepts in various ways, social learning being considered as more effective than individual learning.

The importance of dialogue

Twenty-first century pedagogy foregrounds more frequent use of dialogue in the classroom. Pupils are encouraged to talk more, in collaboration with their peers. This talk requires frequent use of new terms to facilitate pupil understanding and use of conceptual ideas, such as democracy, evaporation or timbre. Observing teacher-talk in cotaught classrooms models this.

Critical thinking and collaborative problem solving

In twentieth century schools, learning was mostly reactive to the teacher, but twenty-first century pedagogy requires collaborative problem solving and investigation by teacher and pupils. The critical approach to linking theory and practice adopted by coteachers can be extended to the pupils in class, so that pupils can help teachers design learning environments that are most effective.

Teaching the unknown

One of the most important aspects of twenty-first century pedagogy is the emphasis on teaching the unknown, not the known. Pupils can access so much information at their fingertips; it is vital in the 'knowledge age' that we create new knowledge, via creative and imaginative approaches in pedagogy. Two different teachers coteaching together bring more potential for developing creative approaches to pupil learning.

Conclusion

The research presented in this book shows that modern classrooms provide significant challenges for new teachers, and introduces coteaching as a way to give high quality, in-class support to PSTs. The evidence indicates that coteaching helps PSTs become much more confident in the classroom from working side by side with experienced professional teachers and, in most cases, leads to higher performance in their school experience assessments. Coteaching PSTs also tend to become more collaborative and confident teachers when they enter the profession, seeking out colleagues to work with in a range of problem-solving situations (Juck et al, 2010). Coteaching supports strategies to reduce the attrition rate of new teachers. It brings benefits also to ISTs; it presents them with excellent CPD in terms of expanding their teaching repertoires, developing mentoring skills and supporting the use of new theories and innovations in their teaching.

We need a new generation of teachers who can develop and foster twenty-first century pedagogical approaches to equip pupils well for the world of work they will enter on leaving school and college. The higher-order skills employers require involves changes to the more traditional ways that pupils are taught. In order for this to occur, substantial development in teacher education is called for. Coteaching is one way to support such change. Bringing ISTs and PSTs together, via an induction process (described in Chapter 4) to coteach for as few as eight lessons is an innovation that can effect significant improvements for both, as well improving pupil enjoyment and attainment in learning.

IN A **NUTSHELL**

» Twenty-first century pedagogy requires a shift from traditional didactic teaching to one which involves pupils and teachers in a collaborative endeavour to use knowledge, not to store it.

» Coteaching supports the development of twenty-first century skills by modelling collaborative ways of learning and by creating dialogical and imaginative tasks which help pupils to engage in collaborative problem solving.

» Coteaching also supports the new ideas of conceptual learning, in which pupils learn with, as well as from, their teachers.

» Coteaching can be considered as a twenty-first century pedagogy for teacher education.

REFLECTIONS ON **CRITICAL ISSUES**

This final chapter has illustrated briefly some of the changes that are beginning to take place in education contexts to foster learning for the 'knowledge age'. It shows that coteaching, as well as the other outcomes summarised in the previous chapter, can play a highly positive role in helping to make these changes happen smoothly. The expectation is for the PSTs to be well-equipped in twenty-first century pedagogical approaches in college and for these to be implemented critically and carefully via coteaching by PSTs and ISTs. It is the ISTs who will be in the position of adapting new approaches so that they can be effective in class. Together, the coteaching PSTs and ISTs can develop ideal learning environments by sharing expertise not only among themselves, but also with pupils and other colleagues.

APPENDIX 1 | EXEMPLAR COTEACHING CODE OF PRACTICE FOR PSTS AND ISTS

As a PST coteacher, I expect to approach coteaching professionally and responsibly by:

» co-operating harmoniously with my IST coteacher(s), particularly during coplanning, implementation and coreflection of lessons;

» protecting and enhancing the good reputation of both the school and the university college;

» contacting my coteacher and school at the earliest opportunity should there be any change in arrangements;

» always attending class punctually;

» keeping a log of classroom experiences during the coteaching period;

» contributing purposefully to all class and group activities;

» being prepared to discuss my classroom experiences with a project researcher;

» seeking advice from my coteachers and tutors as appropriate;

» being equitable in respect of age, gender, race, religion, disability and sexual orientation;

» being confidential when appropriate.

As a coteaching IST, I will endeavour to:

» co-operate harmoniously with colleagues and PSTs throughout the coteaching period;

» keep a log of my classroom experiences during the coteaching period;

» take all reasonable steps to ensure that where alterations to timetabled classes are necessary, these are communicated to PSTs at the earliest opportunity;

» provide PSTs with appropriate classroom support, resources and facilities;

» provide PSTs with appropriate information regarding schemes of work and individual pupil needs;

» provide appropriate feedback to PSTs on their developing teaching skills;

» be prepared to discuss classroom experiences with a project researcher;

» be equitable in respect of age, gender, race, religion, disability and sexual orientation.

Signed:

IST _____ PST _____

APPENDIX 2 | POSSIBLE COTEACHING SCENARIOS

For each scenario, consider your strategies for: (a) that day; and (b) future planning.

1. The IST and PST coteachers have planned a science investigation to take place. The IST is absent on that day – the PST arrives and a supply teacher is in class.

   (a)

   (b)

2. The IST and PST have planned a science investigation. The PST phones in sick on that day.

   (a)

   (b)

3. You are both finding it difficult to make time for coplanning and coreflection of the lesson.

   (a)

   (b)

4. You feel that you are not communicating freely and effectively as coteachers, so the coplanning does not include both voices equally.

   (a)

   (b)

5. After a week or two you feel that something is not quite right in your relationship with the IST/ PST.

   (a)

   (b)

Use the following guide in your coreflection discussions to ensure that you address each of the levels below.

Level 1:   *Surface reflection* (eg: using evidence and making adjustments based on experience only);

Level 2:   *Pedagogical reflection* (eg: adjust methods and practices based on students' relative performance);

Level 3:   Critical pedagogical reflection (eg: commitment to continuous learning and improved practice; constructive criticism of own practice; sees teaching practices as remaining open to further investigation).

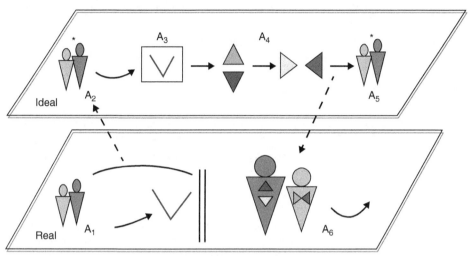

Figure A4.1 KEY:

A1 = agent of activity (coteachers in the 'real' plane, such as the classroom)

V = developmental gap (eg situation in lesson needed to be improved)

A2 = reflective stop (coteachers move into the 'ideal' plane, away from the classroom, as they reflect on the developmental gap, V)

A3 = analysis of situation and choice of mediational means (represented as coloured triangles) such as books, other teachers, tutors, other resources)

A4 = modelling of mediational tools (to construct a practical way of addressing the developmental gap)

A5 = transformation of the model into practical action back in the classroom (real plane)

A6 – reflexive control over the performance of a new practical action

NB The arrow to the right-hand side of A6 represents the next reflective cycle if further refinement is required.

REFERENCES

Bacharach, N, Heck, T and Dahlberg, K (2007) *Collaboratively Researching the Impact of a Coteaching Model of Student Teaching*. Paper presented at the annual meeting of the American Educational Research Association, Chicago.

Bacharach, N, Heck, T W and Dahlberg, K (2010a) Changing the Face of Student Teaching through Coteaching. *Action in Teacher Education*, 32: 3–14.

Bacharach, N, Heck, T and Dahlberg, K (2010b) Researching the Use of Co-teaching in the Student Teaching Experience, in Murphy, C and Scantlebury, K (eds) *Coteaching in International Contexts: Research and Practice* (pp 35–52). Dordrecht: Springer Publishing.

Bandura, A (1977) Self-efficacy: Toward a Unifying Theory of Behavioral Change. *Psychological Review*, 84(2): 191–215.

Beers, J (2005) The Role of Coteaching in the Development of the Practices of an Urban Science Teacher, in Roth, W-M and Tobin, K (eds) *Teaching Together, Learning Together* (pp 79–95). New York: Peter Lang.

Beggs, J, Murphy, C and Kerr, K (2008) *New Approaches to Primary Science Teaching and Assessment.* Report for AstraZeneca Science Teaching Trust.

Bereiter, C (2013) Principled Practical Knowledge: Not a Bridge but a Ladder. *Journal of the Learning Sciences*, 23(1), 4–17. doi: 10.1080/10508406.2013.812533.

Bianchi, L and Murphy, C (2014) *Confidence through Collaboration: Coteaching as a Model of Continuous Professional Development between Primary Science Teachers and STEM Researchers*. Paper presented at 5th International Symposium for Engineering Education, 2014, The University of Manchester. [online] Available at: http://epsassets.manchester.ac.uk/medialand/fascinate/publications/1confidence-through-coteaching.pdf (accessed July 2016).

Carambo, C and Stickney, C T (2009) Coteaching Praxis and Professional Service Facilitating the Transition of Beliefs and Practices. *Cultural Studies of Science Education*, 4: 433–41. doi:10.1007/s11422-008-9148-3.

Carlisle, K (2008) *Coteaching: Role of the Student Teacher in Schools*. PhD thesis, Queen's University Belfast.

Carlisle, K (2010) Enactment of Coteaching in Primary Schools: Moving Towards a Shared Responsibility, in Murphy, C and Scantlebury, K (eds) *Coteaching in International Contexts: Research and Practice* (pp 129–150). Dordrecht: Springer Publishing.

Council for the Curriculum, Examinations and Assessment (CCEA) (2007) *The Northern Ireland Curriculum Primary.* Belfast: CCEA.

Darling-Hammond, L and McLaughlin, M W (1995) Policies That Support Professional Development in an Era of Reform. *Phi Delta Kappan*, 76(8): 597–604.

Dewey, J (1929) The Sources of a Science of Education. *The Kappa Delta Pi Lecture Series*. New York: Horace Liveright, pp 72–77.

Duncombe, R and Armour, K M (2004) Collaborative Professional Learning: From Theory to Practice. *Journal of In-service Education*, 30(1): 141–66.

Eick, C and Ware, F (2005) Coteaching in a Science Methods Course: An Apprenticeship Model for Early Induction to the Secondary Classroom, in Roth, W-M and Tobin, K (eds) *Teaching Together, Learning Together* (pp 187–206). New York: Peter Lang.

Eick, C, Ware, F and Williams, P (2003) Coteaching in a Science Methods Course: A Situated Learning Model of Becoming a Teacher. *Journal of Teacher Education*, 54(1): 74–85.

Gallimore, R, Tharp, R G and John-Steiner, V (1992) *The Developmental and Sociocultural Foundations of Mentoring*. Columbia University, New York: Inst. for Urban Minority Education.

Gallo-Fox, J (2010) Risk-taking as Practice in a Coteaching Professional Learning Community, in Murphy, C and Scantlebury, K (eds) *Coteaching in International Contexts: Research and Practice* (pp 105–24). Dordrecht: Springer Publishing.

Gallo-Fox, J, Wassell, B A, Scantlebury, K and Juck, M (2006) Warts and All: Ethical Dilemmas in Implementing the Coteaching Model. *Forum Qualitative Sozialforschung / Forum: Qualitative Social Research* [Online journal], 7(4*).* [online] Available at: www.qualitative-research.net/index.php/fqs/article/view/183 (accessed July 2016*).*

Garet, M S, Porter, A C, Desimone, L, Birman, B F and Suk Yoon, K (2001) What Makes Professional Development Effective? Results from a National Sample of Teachers. *American Educational Research Journal*, 38(4): 915–45.

Gilbert, J (2005) *Catching the Knowledge Wave? The Knowledge Society and the Future of Education.* Wellington: NZCER Press.

Gleason, S, Fennemore, K and Scantlebury, K (2006) Choreographing Teaching: Co-teaching with Special Education/Inclusion Teachers in Science Classrooms, in Tobin, K (ed) *Teaching and Learning Science: A Handbook* (pp 235–38). New York: Praeger Publishing.

Greenwood, J G, Greenwood, J D, McCullagh, J F, Beggs, J and Murphy, C (2007) A Survey of Sidedness in Northern Irish Schoolchildren: The Interaction of Sex, Age and Task. *Laterality*, 12(1): 1–18.

Harrison, C, Hofstein, A, Eylon, B-S and Simon, S (2008) Evidence-Based Professional Development of Science Teachers in Two Countries. *International Journal of Science Education*, 30(5): 577–91.

Hirsh, S (2009) A New Definition. *Journal of Staff Development*, 30(4): 10–16.

Holzman, L (2010) Without Creating ZPDs There Is No Creativity, in Connery, C John-Steiner, V and Marjanovic-Shane, A (eds) *Dancing with the Muses: A Cultural-Historical Activity Theory Approach to Play, Meaning making, and Creativity* (pp 27–40). New York: Peter Lang Publishers.

Johnston, K, Murchan, D, Loxley, A, Fitzgerald, H and Quinn, M (2007) The Role and Impact of the Regional Curriculum Support Service in Irish Primary Education. *Irish Educational Studies*, 26(3): 219–38.

Juck, M, Scantlebury, K and Gallo-Fox, J (2010) Now It's Time to Go Solo: First Year Teaching, in Murphy, C and Scantlebury, K (eds) *Coteaching in International Contexts: Moving Forward and Broadening Perspectives* (pp 241–61). Dordrecht: Springer Publishing.

Kerin, M and Murphy, C (2015) Exploring the Impact of Coteaching on Preservice Music Teachers. *Asia-Pacific Journal of Teacher Education*, 43(4): 309–23.

Kerr, K (2010) 'It certainly taught us how to change our minds on teaching science': Coteaching in Continuing Professional Development, in Murphy, C and Scantlebury, K (eds) *Coteaching in International Contexts Research and Practice* (pp 147–67). Dordrecht: Springer Publishing.

Korthagen, F A, and Kessels, J P (1999) Linking Theory and Practice: Changing the Pedagogy of Teacher Education. *Educational Researcher*, 28(4): 4–17.

Kyriacou, C and Stephens, P (1999) Student Teachers' Concerns on Teaching Practice. *Evaluation and Research in Education*, 13(1): 18–31.

Lampert-Shepel, E (1999) Reflective Thinking in Educational Praxis: Analysis of Multiple Perspectives. *Educational Foundations*, 13(3): 69–88.

Larrivee, B (2008) Development of a Tool to Assess Teachers' Level of Reflective Practice. *Reflective Practice*, 9: 341–60. doi:10.1080/14623940802207451.

Lave, J. (1988) *Cognition in Practice: Mind, Mathematics, and Culture in Everyday Life*. Cambridge, UK: Cambridge University Press.

Lewis, C, Perry, R and Murata, A (2006) How Should Research Contribute to Instructional Improvement: A Case of Lesson Study. *Educational Researcher*, 35(3): 3–14.

Lyotard, J-F (1984) *The Postmodern Condition: A Report on Knowledge*. Manchester: Manchester University Press.

Martin, S (2009a) Learning to Teach Science, in Tobin, K and Roth, W-M (eds) *World of Science Education: North America* (pp 567–86). Rotterdam: Sense Publishers.

Martin, S (2009b) What Is Necessary, May Not Be Sufficient: An Analysis of Collaborative Models for Learning to Teach Science, in Tobin, K and Roth, W-M (eds) *World of Science Education: North America*. The Netherlands: Sense Publishers.

McLaren, P (2014) *Life in Schools: An Introduction to Critical Pedagogy and the Foundations of Education*, 6th edn. Boulder, CO: Paradigm Publishers.

Murphy, C and Beggs, J (2005) Coteaching as an Approach to Enhance Science Learning and Teaching in Primary Schools, in Roth,W-M and Tobin, K (eds) *Teaching Together, Learning Together* (pp 207–31). New York, NY: Peter Lang.

Murphy, C and Beggs, J (2006) Addressing Ethical Dilemmas in Implementing Coteaching. *Forum Qualitative Sozialforschung / Forum: Qualitative Social Research* [online journal], 7(4), Art. 20. Available at: www.qualitative-research.net/fqs-texte/4–06/06-4-20-e.htm (accessed July 2016).

Murphy, C and Beggs, J (2010) A Five-Year Systematic Study of Coteaching Science in 120 Primary Schools (pp 11–34), in Murphy, C and Scantlebury, K (eds) *Coteaching in International Contexts: Research and Practice* (pp 105–24). Dordrecht: Springer Publishing.

Murphy, C and Carlisle, K (2008) Can They Go It Alone? Addressing Criticism of Coteaching. *Cultural Studies in Science Education*, 4(2): 461–75. doi:10.1007/s1142200891509.

Murphy, C, Beggs, J and Carlisle, K (2004) Students as 'Catalysts' in the Classroom: The Impact of Co-teaching between Science Student Teachers and Primary Classroom Teachers on Children's Enjoyment and Learning of Science. *International Journal of Science Education*, 26(8): 1023–35.

Murphy, C, Beggs, J and Carlisle, K (2007) *New Approaches to Primary Science Teaching and Assessment* (NAPSTA). Final Report. London: AstraZeneca Science Teaching.

Murphy, C, McCullagh, J and Doherty, A (2014) Piloting a model for coteaching. [online] Available at: www.aera.net/Publications/Online-Paper-Repository/AERA-Online-Paper-Repository/Owner/941006/Default (accessed June 2015).

New Zealand Council for Education and Research (NZCER) (no date) Shifting to twenty-first century thinking in education and learning. [online] Available at: www.shiftingthinking.org/?page_id=53. (accessed July 2016).

Nilsson, P (2015) Catching the Moments – Coteaching to Stimulate Science in the Preschool Context. *Asia-Pacific Journal of Teacher Education*, 43(4): s. 296–308.

O'Conaill, N (2010) A Learning Space: Student Teachers' Experiences of Coteaching Science, in Murphy, C and Scantlebury, K (eds) *Coteaching in International Contexts* (pp 173–197). Dordrecht: Springer Publishing.

O'Murchu, F (2011) Team-teaching for inclusive learning: Purposes, practices and perceptions of a team-teaching initiative in Irish post-primary schools. PhD thesis. [online] Available at: https://cora.ucc.ie/bitstream/handle/10468/549/OMurchuF_PhD2011.pdf?sequence=1andisAllowed=y (accessed June 2016).

OECD (2015) Teaching in Focus, 10: Embedding teacher professional development in school for teacher success. [online] Available at: www.oecd-ilibrary.org/docserver/download/5js4rv7s7snt.pdf?expires=1466965120&id=id&accname=guest&checksum=F1B8DDAA5477C94B3393311E4D4DAA60 (accessed June 2016).

Pennsylvania Department of Education (PDE) (2000) Nine Design Principles of Effective Professional Development. *Psychological Review*, 84(2): 191–215.

Rodrigues, S, Marks, A and Steel, P (2003) Developing Science and ICT Pedagogical Content Knowledge: A Model of Continuing Professional Development. *Innovations in Education and Teaching International*, 40(4): 386–94.

Roth, W-M (1998) Science Teaching as Knowledgeability: A Case Study of Knowing and Learning during Coteaching. *Science Education*, 82: 357–77.

Roth, W-M and Tobin, K (2002) *At the Elbow of Another: Learning to Teach by Coteaching*. New York: Peter Lang.

Roth, W-M (2005) Becoming Like the Other, in Roth, W-M and Tobin, K (eds) *Teaching Together, Learning Together* (pp 27–51). New York: Peter Lang.

Roth, W-M and Boyd, N (1999) Coteaching, as Colearning, in Practice. *Research in Science Education*, 29: 51–67.

Roth, W-M and Tobin, K (2001) Learning to Teach Science as Practice. *Teaching and Teacher Education*, 17: 741–62.

Roth, W-M and Tobin, K (2004) Coteaching: From Praxis to Theory. *Teachers and Teaching: Theory and Practice*, 10(2): 161–79.

Roth, W-M and Tobin, K (2005) Coteaching: From Praxis to Theory, in Roth, W-M and Tobin, K (eds) *Teaching Together, Learning Together* (vol 294, pp 1–21). New York: Peter Lang.

Roth, W-M and Tobin, K (2006) *Teaching Together, Learning Together*. New York: Peter Lang.

Roth, W-M, Masciotra, D and Boyd, N (1999) Becoming-in-the-classroom: A Case Study of Teacher Development through Coteaching. *Teaching and Teacher Education*, 15: 771–84.

Scantlebury, K, Gallo-Fox, J and Wassell, B (2008) Coteaching as a Model for Preservice Secondary Science Teacher Education. *Teaching and Teacher Education*, 24: 967–81.

Shaffer, L S and Thomas-Brown, K (2015) Enhancing Teacher Competency through Co-teaching and Embedded Professional Development. *Journal of Education and Training Studies*, 3(3): 117–25.

Shulman, L S (1986) Those Who Understand: Knowledge Growth in Teaching. *Educational Researcher*, 15(2): 4–14.

Shultze, F (2015) A way of teaching and learning. Blog. [online] Accessed at: http://bloggar.ur.se/larlabbet/2015/12/05/ett-satt-att-lara-och-lara-ut/ (accessed July 2016).

Siry, C A (2001) Emphasizing Collaborative Practices in Learning to Teach: Coteaching and Cogenerative Dialogue in a Field-based Methods Course. *Teaching Education*, 22(1): 91–101.

Soffel, J (2016) What are the 21st-century skills every student needs? [online] Available at: www.weforum.org/agenda/2016/03/21st-century-skills-future-jobs-students/ (accessed July 2016).

Stetsenko, A. (2008) From Relational Ontology to Transformative Activist Stance in Conceptualizing Development and Learning: Expanding Vygotsky's (CHAT) Project. *Cultural Studies of Science Education*, 3: 471–91.

Stith, I and Roth, W-M (2006) Who Gets to Ask the Questions: The Ethics in/of Cogenerative Dialogue Praxis [paragraph 46]. *Forum Qualitative Sozialforschung/Forum: Qualitative Social Research*, 7(2), Article 38. [online] Available at: www.qualitative-research.net/fqs-texte/2–06/06-2-38-e.htm (accessed July 2016).

Teaching Council (2013) *Report of the Review Committee on the Bachelor in Music Education*. Maynooth: Teaching Council of Ireland.

Tharp, R G (1993) The Institutional and Social Context of Educational Practice and Reform, in Forman, E A, Minick, N and Stone, C A (eds) *Contexts for Learning: Sociocultural Dynamics in Children's Development* (pp 269–82). Cambridge: Cambridge University Press.

Tharp, R G and Gallimore, R (1988) *Rousing Minds to Life: Teaching, Learning, and Schooling in Social Context*. New York: Cambridge University Press.

Tobin, K (2006) Learning to Teach through Coteaching and Cogenerative Dialogue. *Teaching Education*, 17(2): 133–42.

Tobin, K, Roth, W-M and Zimmermann, A (2001) Learning to Teach Science in Urban Schools. *Journal of Research in Science Teaching*, 38(8): 941–64.

Tobin, K and Roth, W-M (2005a) Coteaching/Cogenerative Dialoguing in an Urban Science Teacher Preparation Programme, in Roth, W-M and Tobin, K (eds) *Teaching Together, Learning Together* (pp 59–77). New York: Peter Lang.

Tomlinson, P (1995) *Understanding Mentoring: Reflective Strategies for School-based Teacher Preparation*. Buckingham: Open University Press.

Upadhyay, B and Gifford, A (2011) Changing Lives: Coteaching Immigrant Students in a Middle School Science Classroom, in Murphy, C and Scantlebury, K (eds) *Coteaching in International Contexts: Research and Practice* (pp 267–83). Dordrecht: Springer Publishing.

Vygotsky, L S (1931/1997) *The History of the Development of Higher Mental Functions* (Hall, M J Trans.), in Rieber, R W (ed) *The Collected Works of L. S. Vygotsky. Volume 4: The History of the Development of Higher Mental Functions* (pp 1–251). New York: Plenum Press.

Vygotsky, L S (1934/1987) *Thinking and Speech*, in Rieber, R W and Carton, A S (eds) *The Collected Works of L. S. Vygotsky* (vol 1, pp 37–285). New York: Plenum.

Vygotsky, L S (1978) *Mind in Society: The Development of Higher Psychological Processes*. Cole, M, John-Steiner, V, Scribner, S and Souberman, E (eds). Cambridge, MA: Harvard University Press.

Weale, S (2015) Four in ten new teachers quit within a year. *Guardian* newspaper. [online] Available at: www.theguardian.com/education/2015/mar/31/four-in-10-new-teachers-quit-within-a-year (accessed July 2016).

Weale, S (2016) Long hours, endless admin and angry parents – why schools just can't get the teachers. *Guardian* newspaper. [online] Available at: www.theguardian.com/education/2016/feb/01/schools-teachers-classroom-crisis-stress-grind (accessed July 2016).

Weisner, T S (1984) Ecocultural Niches of Middle Childhood: A Cross-cultural Perspective, in Collins, W A (ed) *Development during Middle Childhood: The Years from Six to Twelve* (pp 335–69). Washington, DC: National Academy of Sciences Press.

Willis, L and Ritchie, S (2010) Parents as Coteachers of Science and Technology in a Middle School Classroom, in Murphy, C and Scantlebury, K (eds) *Coteaching in International Contexts: Research and Practice* (pp 285–306). Dordrecht: Springer Publishing.

INDEX